HIDDEN
HISTORY
of
MOBILE

Joe Cuhaj

THE
History
PRESS

Published by The History Press
Charleston, SC
www.historypress.com

Front cover: "Old Stove Roundup." *Mobile Public Library Digital Collections.*

First published 2020

Manufactured in the United States

ISBN 9781467143547

Library of Congress Control Number: 2019951266

This book is dedicated to my daughter, Kellie, and her love of history, proving that the apple doesn't fall far from the tree—while also proving Sir Isaac Newton's unwritten law, don't sit under apple trees.

CONTENTS

Contents

Acknowledgements

Writing a history book like this involves spending a lot of time with dead people, but they have a voice and I can't thank all of the wonderful historians, museum staff and curators, journalists and educators enough for taking the time to help give these people that voice and for answering my endless questions. They went out of their way to point me in the right direction to find some obscure details of Mobile's rich history. Special thanks go to the curator of the Mobile Carnival Museum, Cartledge W. Blackwell III; Mobile Municipal Cemeteries manager Hereford Marston; Tracy Neely and all of the members of the Mobile Creole Cultural and Historical Preservation Society; University of Alabama professor Guy Hubbs; director of the History Museum of Mobile Meg McCrummen Fowler and assistant research historian Lindy White; Valerie Ellis with the Local History and Genealogy Department of the Mobile Public Library; my daughter, Kellie, and her husband, Michael Dorie, for answering tricky questions about Elvis and pointing the way to some hidden history of Mobile Bay and the delta; and my wife, Maggie, for digging through the archives in search of the lost. Thank you all.

INTRODUCTION

There are two things I absolutely love. First of all, I love to tell stories—short nonfiction and humorous fictional stories, stories about our environment and wildlife, stories about everyday people. My second love is history, but not just your everyday, run-of-the-mill you can find it in any textbook history, but hidden history—lesser-known facts about people or events that have been lost in the mist of time.

But, full disclosure—I am not an historian, nor have I played one on TV. I just have a deep-seated love of history—sifting through dusty archives, gingerly turning the browning pages of well-worn books and going page by page through newspapers in archives. Heck, my DVR is usually overloaded with programs from the History and Smithsonian Channels.

I have been fortunate over the years to have been able to bring those two loves—storytelling and history—together. Whether it's in my many outdoor recreation books, web content or print articles, every story I tell always ends up having some historical aspect that I quite often stumble upon, find fascinating and then embark down that rabbit hole on a trip to flesh it out and bring it to readers. And as I found out when I moved to Mobile almost forty years ago, there is no better place to tell those stories than right here in this three-hundred-plus-year-old port city.

What exactly is "hidden history"? I put that in quotes because it is a very subjective phrase. To me, and for the purposes of this book, I look at it in two ways. The first is the most obvious—truly hidden history, stories from the past that have been completely lost in the mists of time like the

Old meets new: Mobile's third cemetery—Magnolia—beneath the state's tallest skyscraper, the RSA Tower. *Author's collection.*

story of Reverend Shandy Jones or how Harpo Marx obtained his first real harp in Mobile.

Then there is the type of history that appears to be well known, but if you dig down deeper under the surface you will find some interesting twists and turns. For example, as you read through the book, you will undoubtedly see the names of some famous Mobilians whose stories you've probably heard before, like that of Augusta Evans Wilson, the first American female author to earn over $100,000. Many of us know her life story, but the underlying and lesser-known tale is of her propagandist writings for the Confederacy which adds to her legend and will give you a better understanding and perspective of her life.

Either way, my goal is to present some of these hidden historical gems in a way that's not stodgy like your old seventh grade history teacher would, but as a story where I hopefully give life to the event. As you scan the pages you will read a bit of basic textbook Mobile history, but that's only a primer to refresh your memory and give you a little perspective into what lies ahead.

But before we get into the hidden history of the Port City—or Azalea City, as it is also known—you might be asking yourself, what makes Mobile, Alabama, so special? Plenty! As the State of Alabama was celebrating its bicentennial in 2019, Mobile was celebrating its 317th. But the city's history begins way before that, and it's all because of the water.

If you take a look at the Alabama state seal, you will be struck by one thing—it is a wet state. The seal depicts all the major rivers that flow through the state. Over the years, these waterways have been the backbone for the state's economy and growth. Many of those thousands of miles of creeks, rivers and streams flow southward, carrying with them rich nutrients as they join together to form five rivers: the Mobile, Spanish, Tensaw, Apalachee and Blakeley. Taken together, these five rivers create the second-largest river delta in the country, the Mobile-Tensaw. It is here in this rich, fertile environment of veining backwaters and bayous that Native Americans first established themselves thousands of years ago. Tribes like the Alabamu, Tomeh and Mabila lived along the fruited banks in palm-thatched villages or atop towering earthen mounds.

Those rivers continue to flow southward, eventually joining together to form a wide bay that was named for one of those tribes and where the future port city would rise—Mobile Bay. (Mobile is the anglicized version of Mabila.) The city that was built here became a prized possession for several nations: Spanish conquistador Alonso Álvarez de Pineda first explored this land in 1519, engaging with the native tribes and bringing with him devastating European diseases. The French government first settled here in 1702, establishing a ramshackle fort they called Fort Louis de la Louisiane in 1702 on the Mobile River's 27-Mile Bluff, only to move fifteen miles downstream nine years later to where present-day Mobile is located. The British won the settlement following the signing of the Treaty of Paris with France that ended the French and Indian War (also known as the Seven Years' War) in 1763. Spain then claimed the territory after invading it in 1780 only to have it taken away by the United States in 1813.

Since then, Mobile has seen and done it all—created a southern delicacy, gumbo, as well as West Indies Salad. The city is the birthplace of Mardi Gras in America, earning it the title the "Mother of Mystics." During the Civil War, the first operational submarine, the CSS *Hunley*, and its predecessor, the *Pioneer II* (aka *American Diver*) was built here. The city became the last Confederate port city to surrender during that war. It produced five Hall of Fame baseball players, third on the list of all U.S. cities. It's been battered by hurricanes and was a major player in the war effort during World War

II. The list goes on and on and on, so much so that it would take volumes to document it all, and it does.

But that's not for this book. All of that is well-known history. I hope that you will find within these pages nuggets of history that will be enlightening and engaging, stories that will intrigue you and pique your curiosity about the grand history of the Mother of Mystics, the Azalea City, the Port City, Mobile.

It's time to dig in to a little of its hidden history.

THE FIRST MOBILIANS

W hen Charles Delisle sailed up Mobile Bay into the heart of Gulf Coast Indian country in 1700, he discovered a world that seemed to be a paradise. In his log entry on June 19, he wrote:

The river divides into three branches at the boundary of their lands [the Thomees], *and makes two islands which are very beautiful, and deserted in several places. This place is adorned with beautiful peach trees that are covered in fruit, but I do not know the quality they are since they were still green. There are also grapes which cover the banks of the river.*

This was one of the earliest descriptions by a European of the 250,000-acre Mobile-Tensaw River delta, the second largest in the country. The delta is formed and maintained by the funneling of water runoff from across the Southeast down a myriad of creeks, streams and tributaries where they merge into five separate rivers—the Mobile, Spanish, Tensaw, Apalachee, and Blakeley—that eventually join together to create Mobile Bay. The water then flows southward into the Gulf of Mexico.

The nutrients that are brought down over these thousands of miles of waterways make the delta a rich and fertile land, teeming with wildlife and rare plants. While the delta is no longer the paradise described by Charles Delisle, it is still an amazing wonderland of bottomland forest, brackish tidal marshes, cypress-gum swamps and floodplain, making this one of the largest intact wetlands remaining in the country, and it's located right on the city of Mobile's doorstep.

The variety of wildlife that lives within this wonderland is amazing in and of itself—alligators, blue heron, black bear, any number of snake species, wild boar. It is this diversity, this rich environment that brought human habitation to the region in the first place. These people can rightfully be called the first Mobilians, their settlement dating to around AD 1000, a time known as the Mississippian period.

Today, the delta resembles a South American rainforest and is referred to as "America's Amazon." The long, snaking bayous and backwaters are lined with towering cypress trees and row upon row of saw palmetto. Buried deep within this environment you will find evidence of the Mississippians of Mobile on a small island called Mound Island.

The Mississippian period was a time when Indian tribes were settling along the Mississippi River and then slowly migrated outward, settling into other areas of the Southeast, including the Mobile-Tensaw delta, around the year 1250. What made Mississippians unique is their skill in building earthen mounds, and not just any tiny hill, either. Here on Mound Island, eighteen mounds were built all by hand. The mounds were created by digging dirt with shell hoes from "borrow pits" either on the island itself or on shore, then carrying baskets of the dirt by hand one at a time to the mound's location. It took hundreds of years to complete all of the mounds on Mound Island.

The tallest mound on the island, what archaeologists call Mound A, was reserved for the chief to live on and look down over the tribe. The next tallest, Mound B, was for the religious leader. This mound is not as tall as the chief's mound, but it is long—about the length of a football field. Mid-size mounds were for the upper middle class, and all the workers lived at ground level.

While there are many other Mississippian mounds scattered about the Southeast, like those found at Moundville near Tuscaloosa, Alabama, Mound Island appears to have been the tribe's spiritual capital. French colonist Pierre Le Moyne d'Iberville wrote that the island was "where the Gods are" and tribes would come here to offer sacrifices.

You can visit the mounds of Mound Island today. The island was declared a National Historic Site in 1995, but it is a difficult trek. There are two ways to get there. The first is by kayak, but you need to be an experienced paddler with excellent navigational skills. (The delta is a dangerous place, and many people get lost in its bayous). The second is by taking one of the many tour boats. Often a historian accompanies the ride and will give you a detailed history of the island. Visitors are able to climb to the top of the chief's

An example of a Native American mound near Tuscaloosa. An identical mound can be found deep in the heart of the Mobile-Tensaw River delta. *Author's collection.*

mound, Mound A. Check out the Alabama Historical Commission's website for trip schedules at ahc.alabama.gov.

From the Mississippian period, other Native Americans began to filter into the region and thrived with the abundance of food available. One of those tribes was named Mabila, a word that means "paddlers" (although some archaeologists and historians call the tribe Mauvilla or Maubila). It is believed that the people were Choctaw. Later, the name would be anglicized to become Mobile.

The first European contact with the tribe came in 1519 when Spanish explorer Alonso Álvarez de Pineda sailed up Mobile Bay and the Mobile River as he continued his mission to map the Gulf of Mexico. Spain believed that the tribe was a "great empire" that covered the entire central south region of the Gulf. The natives' language, Mobilian, was basically the English of the day and was spoken throughout the region.

While that first meeting was cordial, the next was far from that. Spanish explorer Hernando de Soto and his crew crisscrossed the Southeast on a mission—to ferret out all of the gold and treasure in the region for himself.

After setting up camp in Tallahassee in 1539, de Soto led his six-hundred-plus troops westward, kidnapping native warriors and forcing them to guide his crew to other villages and—hopefully—the gold he coveted. Most of the time, the guides misled de Soto, taking him well off course to avoid the larger villages.

The following year, the expedition entered the region that would later become Alabama and met Chief Tuskaloosa. After the chief refused to voluntarily carry the expedition's supplies, de Soto captured the man and forced him into being a guide. Tuskaloosa pointed out that there was a town nearby under his control where the tribesmen would be glad to help the explorer.

The now captured chief led the expedition to the village of Mabila where thousands of Indians lay in wait. When an advanced guard of de Soto's expedition arrived in the village on October 18, 1540, the heavily armored Spaniards were taken by surprise as the warriors came out of hiding, and with that, the bloodiest battle to ever take place on North American soil between Europeans and Native Americans began. By the time the dust settled, the Spaniards had lost 20 men with 250 wounded. The tribe, however, was devastated. Estimates have their losses between 5,000 and 6,000. This defeat, as well as the spread of diseases brought to the region by the Europeans, decimated the tribe. De Soto never did find his riches and died after crossing the Mississippi due to fever in 1542.

The site of the Battle of Mabila has never been found. It was believed to have been close to where present-day Mobile is located, but excavations have disproven that theory. Archaeologists are currently looking in Clarke County, about one hundred miles north of Mobile. Whoever discovers the site will be the finder of what is referred to as the "Holy Grail of Southern Archaeology."

Fast-forward once again to 1700 as Delisle and four Canadians began their journey in a bark canoe through the Mobile-Tensaw River delta. Delisle recorded in his journal, *Voyage de M. de Sauvole dufort des Bilochies ou Maurepas aux Thomies, sur la Mobile a trente-six lieues de distance*, that he had met with a tribesman from the Mabila tribe who told him that there were thirty-six separate tribes along the delta's shores, including one called the Alibamou (sometimes spelled Alebamon or Alabamu), from which the state's name was derived.

As for the remaining Mabila, Delisle estimated the population was around five hundred. The tribe lived in five separate villages along one of the delta's rivers. Each village had cabins with high, earthen walls and thatched roofs made of palm leaves that were anchored to the structure with split cane.

Spanish explorer Hernando de Soto made his mark on Mobile during the Battle of Mabila. *Library of Congress, Prints and Photographs Division.*

He described the men as being skilled bow hunters. Their prey was turkey, bear, deer and, yes, buffalo. In general, the people Delisle encountered were of "strong, merry temperament; they dance and play almost always, but reserve the months of May and June for sowing their maize, beans, squash, and watermelons which are their year round food."

From that description, it almost sounds as if the first Mobilians, the Mabila, already had the celebration spirit long before present-day Mobile celebrated the first Mardi Gras.

2

FILLES À LA CASSETTE

The Pelican Girls

The first French settlement in what was to later become Mobile was established in 1702 by Jean-Baptiste Le Moyne de Bienville and his brother, Pierre Le Moyne d'Iberville, after their colony in Biloxi was overcome by a yellow fever epidemic. This first settlement was not located where present-day Mobile can be found. Instead, it was fifteen miles north from that site on a clay bluff overlooking the Mobile River that became known as 27-Mile Bluff. This first settlement, a crude fort to say the least, was named for the king of France—Fort Louis de la Louisiane.

France's King Louis XIV had plans to make this new and wild territory into the next great French colony, but the early explorers found life along the Gulf Coast to be harsh due to the heat, humidity, alligators and mosquitoes, making working the land difficult. And it didn't help that many of the colonists were under the misconception that there were vast riches to be had along the region's bayous and backwaters. They would rather dream of amassing a fortune in gold so that they could return to France and live a life of luxury than work the land and grow crops in order to survive.

Those treasures were never found, and instead of living indolent lives of luxury, the colonists had to find ways to simply survive. The colonists either had to rely on trading with Indian tribes for food or they would have to wait for supply ships to arrive from France with fresh supplies, which were often delayed or didn't arrive at all. Bienville complained several times to the marine minister, Jean-Frédéric Phélypeaux, comte de Pontchartrain (an administrator of sorts for the new colonies), about the idle colonists, warning him that they would be the downfall of the new French settlements. Bienville's warnings went unheeded, and before long, the colonists began to feel the emptiness and pains of famine. But food wasn't the colony's only problem. With a few notable exceptions, the colony was composed of men, and you can't populate and form a sustainable population without women—"suitable" women, as Bienville called them.

Bienville recognized that this would be an issue from the moment the explorers first set foot on the Gulf Coast. Every year since their arrival, Bienville wrote to the king explaining the situation. In one of his letters he asserted:

> *If you want to make something of this country, it is absolutely necessary to send this year some families and a few girls who will be married off shortly after arrival.*

The king relented and agreed to begin the recruitment of women to be brides for the new colonists. He had dealt with this same situation in the past when France colonized the island of Martinique in the Caribbean. He had sent a contingent of women to the island to marry the colonists, but the women selected had "questionable" backgrounds and often refused to marry once they arrived. To the king, these women were not pious or submissive enough, and that mistake would not be made again. He decided that the women would have to be virgins with no family or prospects for the future.

This time around, the king tasked the Catholic Church with the job of canvassing the convents throughout France to find women whose character was beyond reproach. The girls were promised a new life in a land of paradise and a chance to marry the brave French patriots in the new colony.

Letters of recommendation were required to participate in the selection process, with the "finalists" having to go through a rigorous set of examinations to verify that they held the highest of moral values.

Finally, in October 1703, twenty-three young women ranging in age from fourteen to nineteen climbed aboard carriages along with escorts and traveled three hundred miles from Paris to Rochefort, France, where they would set sail on the three-month-long voyage aboard the vessel *Pelican*. These girls were known by many names. Some called the women *filles à la Cassette*, or "Cassette Girls." Still others referred to them as *Casquette* or "Casket Girls," a name that came from the small wooden boxes containing a few essentials the girls would need to start life in the new settlement that the French government had given them. The first girls to arrive in Mobile were known by the name of the ship they sailed on—the Pelican Girls.

A woodcut of the Pelican Girls arriving on the Gulf Coast in 1704. *Public domain.*

Upon the ship's departure, the French government wrote to Bienville:

> *His majesty sends by that ship 20 girls to be married to the Canadians and others who have begun habitations at Mobile in order that this colony can firmly establish itself. Each of these girls was raised in virtue and piety and know how to work, which will render them useful in the colony by showing the Indian girls what they can do, for this there being no point in sending other than of virtue known and without reproach.*

The voyage was not without risk. Many of the girls became ill, and the ship almost capsized in a massive storm before arriving at their first destination, Cap-Haitien, Haiti. From there it was off to Havana, Cuba, where they arrived on July 7, 1704. The bishop of Cuba put the girls up in decent housing, fed them and took them on tours of the city. There was one discomfort, however, that they encountered that would later come back to haunt the women and the settlement they would soon call home—mosquitoes.

The next stop for the *Pelican* was Pensacola, Florida, to resupply, but the Spanish garrison occupying the settlement refused to allow the ship to land. Instead, the *Pelican* was forced to anchor offshore, and the Spaniards sent supplies out to the vessel.

At last, on August 1, 1704, the Pelican Girls arrived at Dauphin Island (then called Massacre Island) at the mouth of Mobile Bay, but before they could begin the final leg of the journey up the bay and Mobile River, the mosquito encounter they had in Havana began to take its toll. Unknown at the time, mosquitoes were the carriers of yellow fever. By the time the *Pelican* landed on the island, half of the crew had died from the disease contracted from the Cuban mosquitoes. Several of the girls also died, and eventually, numerous settlers and Native Americans fell victim to the disease.

An interesting piece of the Pelican Girls story is that the *Pelican* had onboard a fruit that was native to Africa—okra. The word *okra* is a shortened version of the African words *guingombo* or *kingombo*. This shipment of okra was obtained when the *Pelican* landed in the Caribbean on its way to Mobile.

Legend has it that on the girls' arrival, Bienville's housekeeper, Madame Langlois, whipped up a fish stew with some local vegetables in it that the local Indians had grown and taught her how to cook. Langlois added a few touches of her own to the soup, including the French spice filé powder. This is believed to have been the birth of Creole cooking.

The girls loved the stew but thought it needed something extra—okra. And with that, the southern delicacy gumbo was born.

Despite what you might think, the marriages that ensued were not random. The girls came armed with information about the fifty or so available men, including their financial situations and backgrounds, but trouble was afoot not long after the women came ashore.

Once the women arrived, they realized that this was not the Garden of Eden they were promised. Instead, it was a rough collection of ramshackle huts with dirt floors, pools of stagnant water in ditches around the settlement teeming with mosquitoes and food shortages. The men didn't change their ways and continued to refuse to plant crops. The food situation became so bad that the women were relegated to eating Indian corn and acorns.

Disillusioned but determined, the women organized and initiated what has become known as the Petticoat Rebellion. They refused to let the men sleep with them or even live indoors until their housing and food conditions were improved.

The resourceful women won the day and the men got to work, but overall conditions in the new settlement were still appalling and the women made sure that Bienville heard their grievances. Bienville became infuriated with the women, calling them "pampered city girls," and demanded that the king send hardworking country girls next time.

That first month in the settlement saw wedding ceremonies held almost on a daily basis. All of the marriages were conducted by Father LaVente, who had accompanied the girls on the voyage across the Atlantic as a chaperone. All of the girls married except for one, Francoise du Boisrenaud.

In a story told by Wayne Saucier from family records, the king's lieutenant (and cousin of Bienville) Pierre Boisbriant asked the young Francoise du Boisrenaud to marry him. For unknown reasons, Bienville forbade the wedding, and it is said that Bienville tried to force her into marrying another man. She refused, and once again, Bienville became angry. Writing to Pontchartrain, Bienville demanded that Pontchartrain interject himself into the dispute and force Francoise to marry the man Bienville had chosen for her. Pontchartrain denied the request, but even so, for one reason or another, Pierre and Francoise never became husband and wife. Francoise remained in the settlement but never married.

Following the Pelican Girls, several more ships arrived at other French settlements along the Gulf Coast, with more Casket Girls arriving in Biloxi in 1719 and in New Orleans in 1728. Today, many families in Mobile can trace their roots back to the original Pelican Girls.

3

A SHORT HISTORY QUIZ

Before we continue on our journey through some of Mobile's hidden history, let's play a little game. Can you name the fifteen original colonies? Go ahead. Take your time.

No, it's not a trick question. Technically speaking, there were actually fifteen British colonies in North America, not thirteen. How can that be, you ask? Well, here's the story.

We all know that the thirteen originals included (in order of appearance) Virginia, Massachusetts, Maryland, Connecticut, Rhode Island, Delaware, New Hampshire, North Carolina, South Carolina, New Jersey, New York, Pennsylvania and Georgia. But even farther south, there were two more— East and West Florida. The capitals of those two colonies were St. Augustine and Pensacola, respectively. Mobile happened to be on the extreme western side of the West Florida territory.

Between the years 1756 and 1763, France and Great Britain were in the throes of a bloody struggle for territory not only in what would eventually become known as the United States but across Europe and the Caribbean as well. In 1756, France was in control of the western side of the Gulf Coast colony that included Mobile. Spain was in control of the eastern side, or most of Florida.

The Seven Years' War, as it was called in Europe (the French and Indian War in the colonies) was sparked by France's expansion into the Ohio River valley, which brought their territory in direct dispute with the claimed territory of Britain in Virginia.

In the early conflict, British forces routed the French, taking over French Canada as well as all of India and many of the French island colonies in the Caribbean. Spain was eventually drawn into the conflict, as British forces took control of Havana and the island of Cuba. The Spanish monarchy immediately signed a pact, the Family Compact, with France effectively joining the war against Britain. Spain vowed that it would never sign a peace treaty with its archrival if the Spanish crown had to cede Cuba to the British monarchy. Britain, on the other hand, refused to sign a treaty with either country if it couldn't retain what it had thus far fought for and won during the war.

But the war was taking its toll on all belligerents involved, both financially and physically. France and Britain had enough, and informal peace negotiations began in June 1762. On February 10, 1763, the Treaty of Paris was signed. The agreement gave Spanish-controlled Florida to Britain in exchange for Cuba. France was the biggest loser of the war, having to cede several West Indian islands in the Caribbean, all French territory in India and, more importantly for the purposes of this story, all French-controlled territory in North America east of the Mississippi (with the exception of New Orleans) to Britain. The British immediately turned their new possessions along the Gulf Coast into two new colonies: West and East Florida. With that, Mobile officially became a British possession and part of the fifteen original colonies.

The two colonies remained in British possession during the American Revolution, but it was a short-lived victory, as Spain attacked the region and took control of the two territories in 1780, putting Mobile under control of a third European country in less than eighty years.

Scholars do not include East and West Florida as part of the original colonies for the mere fact that these two regions were more sympathetic to the British monarchy than those along the Eastern Seaboard, and of course, Britain lost the land to Spain a few short years after acquiring it. But, for a brief time, Mobile and what is now the state of Florida were part of America's original colonies.

4

THE GREAT RUSSIAN ROYALTY HOAX

In 1711, the Le Moyne brothers made the decision to move the French settlement of Fort Louis de la Louisiane from 27-Mile Bluff on the Mobile River south to what would eventually become the city of Mobile. Living conditions at the bluff were only worsening for the French settlers. There were regular and devastating floods, a lack of food and diseases were running rampant.

Together with local Indian tribes, the French built a small wooden fort at this new location and also named it Fort Louis de la Louisiane, but within ten years, this new structure was in great disrepair. Plans began to evolve for a new earthen brick and stone fort—Fort Conde—that would be built near the current settlement.

It took two more years for construction to begin on the new fort. In the meantime, the settlers were still facing many of the same hardships they faced on the bluff—food shortages, disease, devastating storms, mosquitoes, snakes and alligators. With all of this adversity, why would a member of European royalty flee her homeland and come to this backwater town? But she did, or at least the five hundred settlers at the fort believed she did.

A boatload of two hundred German immigrants bound for the Arkansas River to establish a settlement arrived at the fort in the summer of 1721. From the boat stepped a young woman described as the most beautiful they had ever seen; she was wearing expensive clothing and exquisite jewelry. As the Germans disembarked, they began to whisper to the colonists that the young woman traveling with them was the daughter-in-law of Russia's

The real wife of the son of Peter the Great, Princess Charlotte Christina Sophia, not the imposter who came to Mobile in 1721. *Royal Collection UK.*

Emperor Peter the Great. She had been married to his son, Tsarevich Alexei Petrovich. Her name was Princess Charlotte Christina Sophia. But why would the princess come to Mobile?

Although the young woman said that she was not at liberty to talk about her identity and that she was traveling incognito, the rumor spread that she was, indeed, the princess and that she was fleeing from her husband and his abusive, drunken ways. The story was as riveting as any suspense novel. Just before she was to give birth to her second child, she pretended to be seriously ill and requested that if she were to die, her body should not be embalmed. Shortly after the birth of her son, and with the aid of her royal servants, she faked her death, and per her request, her body was not embalmed. She was placed in a casket and then into a mausoleum. Hours later, the servants opened the casket and helped her flee the country.

There was only one problem with the story. Military leaders in Mobile were suspicious of her claims, since they had heard that the princess had actually died six years earlier in 1715 and that she was buried in St. Petersburg, Russia. Those suspicions were squelched, however, when a young officer at the fort,

Chevalier D'Aubant, said that when he had once visited St. Petersburg, he was introduced to Princess Charlotte. D'Aubant verified that this woman was in fact the princess. The couple married and made a home in Mobile, and not long after, Charlotte gave birth to a baby girl.

In December 1758, D'Aubant was reassigned to Fort Toulouse along the Coosa River in present-day Wetumpka. The chevalier left his wife and daughter in Mobile and began his journey on horseback to the settlement. One year later, Charlotte grew tired of being left alone and longed for her husband. She made the decision to pack up her daughter and a female servant and climbed aboard a boat bound for Fort Toulouse.

It was a long and arduous fifty-day trip up the winding Alabama River. When they arrived, the princess was greeted warmly by both the settlers and the women of the local Native American tribes who would often visit with her and have lengthy conversations. Not wanting his princess bride to sleep in the shabby accommodations within the fort, her husband set about having a special cabin built outside the fort's walls for his family, complete with brick chimney and fireplace.

A few years later, the chevalier was recalled to France and was accompanied by his wife and daughter; they lived abroad until D'Aubant's death in 1765.

But what about the identity of the princess? Was it really Princess Charlotte? Her true identity was exposed when a German nobleman saw the princess as she strolled through the Tuileries Garden in Paris. He immediately recognized her as being the real Princess Charlotte's wardrobe servant. Upon Charlotte's death, the servant had stolen some of her clothing and jewelry. The nobleman reported this to writer François-Marie Arouet (better known by his pen name, Voltaire), who then wrote about it in the local press. Her cover was blown.

The imposter Princess Charlotte died in 1771 in poverty after selling off all of the jewelry. The real Princess Charlotte Christina Sophia did, in fact, die in 1715 after giving birth to a son in St. Petersburg.

5

THE CLANDESTINE MISSION OF AARON BURR

The early recorded history of Mobile can be complicated. It began as the capital of French Louisiana in 1702. It became a prize won by the British following the French and Indian War that ended in 1763 before it was captured by Spain in 1780. It finally came into U.S. possession after being captured by General James Wilkinson and his troops in 1813 and was officially sold to the United States by a treaty with Spain in 1821.

And those are only the highlights. Within that timeline, there were many fascinating twists and turns that eventually made Mobile what it is today; one of those involved the former vice president of the United States, Aaron Burr. But first, a little background.

After the signing of the Treaty of Paris in 1783 effectively ended the American Revolution, the size of the United States nearly doubled with the cessation of land west of the Mississippi River to the fledgling country. The treaty also established additional land agreements between Britain, France, the Netherlands and Spain. For Spain, it meant the acquisition of what was then called East and West Florida, better known today as Baldwin and Mobile County in Alabama and the state of Florida. France retained what was known as the Louisiana Territory, which stretched from the Mississippi River westward to the Rocky Mountains and Canada.

There was only one catch: France believed that Mobile was to be included in the deal, but the United States said otherwise. The United States declared that the port city was not part of the Louisiana Territory negotiated in the Paris treaty, and with this strong backing from the Americans, Spain held on to Mobile. France vehemently protested, but to no avail.

In 1804, a young judge by the name of Harry Toulmin was appointed superior court judge for the Tombigbee District of the Mississippi Territory by President Thomas Jefferson. The Mississippi Territory stretched from the Mississippi River eastward to Georgia and from a line near where Alabama's future capital, Montgomery, would later be established, to the thirty-first parallel, the earth's longitudinal line that crossed only about twenty miles north of Mobile. The territory below this demarcation (which included Mobile) was still under the control of Spain.

The residents of the territory were virtually landlocked and desperately wanted access to the Gulf of Mexico and the Mississippi River for trade, but land retained by Spain stood in their way. Upon his appointment, Toulmin, who supported the United States' annexation of the coastal areas, petitioned Congress to do just that but was denied. He accepted the government's decision and immediately set up his office along that thirty-first parallel at Fort Stoddard right on Spain's doorstep. From here, he set out on a mission—to keep Mobile in the hands of Spain until the United States decided it was time to annex the region.

Three years after Toulmin's appointment, rumors began to fly that a hero of the American Revolution, the former vice president of the United States, the man who killed Secretary of the Treasury Alexander Hamilton in a duel, Aaron Burr, was coming to Mobile with every intention of annexing the Spanish territory to create a new, independent republic—an act of treason as far as the United States was concerned.

Aaron Burr came to Mobile in a failed attempt to annex Spanish-held Mobile into a free and independent country. *Public domain.*

Aaron Burr was a law student in 1775 when he signed up to fight with the Continental army. During his time in service, he became a war hero not once but twice. Burr was credited with saving an entire brigade of soldiers that was trapped in Manhattan by British troops, and later, he squelched a potential mutiny by George Washington's troops facing an extreme northeastern winter at Valley Forge.

Following the war, Burr completed his law degree and began a career in politics; twice elected to the New York State Assembly, he was appointed to the office of New York attorney general and then elected to the U.S. Senate.

It was in the presidential election of 1800 that things took a dramatic turn for the worse for Burr. Thomas Jefferson, John Adams and Burr were duking it out for the presidency. In the country's early elections, candidates did not run on a ticket of president and vice president. Instead, all candidates vied for the presidency, with the runner-up becoming vice president.

As it turned out, Burr went beyond expectations and actually tied Jefferson for office of president. The outcome of the election would be determined by the House of Representatives. The man who would later become the nation's first secretary of the treasury, Alexander Hamilton, took matters into his own hands and began a blistering campaign against Burr that ultimately helped swing the tie-breaking votes in Jefferson's favor, leaving Burr as vice president.

Throughout his first term in office, Jefferson virtually ignored his vice president, leaving him out of important discussions and decisions. When the next election came up, Burr was removed from his position by the president. Once out of office, Burr decided to make a run for governor of New York. During the race, Hamilton appeared again, publicly calling Burr "the most unfit and dangerous man of the community." The smear campaign was effective. With those words, Burr suffered a devastating loss to Morgan Lewis.

Burr was outraged and called out Hamilton publicly. His resentment and hatred grew until he couldn't stand it any longer and challenged Hamilton to a duel.

On the morning of July 11, 1804, the two met in a field in Weehawken, New Jersey, with Burr exacting his vengeance, killing Hamilton.

Fast-forward three years. As the story goes, on a cold February night, a young lawyer from Mobile, Nicholas Perkins, and a friend were playing backgammon in a cabin north of Mobile near Fort Stoddard when they heard the sound of hoofbeats approaching and, soon after, a knock on the door.

Opening the door, Perkins was greeted by a pair of travelers, one of whom he described as wearing ragged pants but "strikingly beautiful boots" As if it were scripted for a dramatic scene, at that moment, the fire in the cabin blazed, giving Perkins a glimpse of the man's face. He noted that it was a noble face with "sparkling eyes."

The travelers asked directions to the nearest tavern. Perkins told them that the nearest one was seven miles down the road. Thanking Perkins, the travelers rode off. Perkins had heard the rumors about Burr and knew the man was wanted for treason. He turned to his friend and said, "That is Aaron Burr. I have read a description of him, and I cannot be mistaken."

He jumped on his horse and galloped off into the night to tell the sheriff. The pair made their way to the tavern, where they confronted the traveler. The sheriff was not as convinced as Perkins was as to the man's identity, but after a lengthy conversation, the sheriff became a believer. He borrowed a canoe and paddled down the Mobile River to Fort Stoddard, where he convinced the fort's commandant, Captain Edward P. Gaines, to put together a detachment of soldiers to arrest the stranger.

As the sun rose the next morning, the detachment met up with the travelers. Gaines stepped up and asked, "I presume, Sir, I have the honor of addressing Colonel Burr?"

The traveler replied, "I am a traveler in the country and do not recognize your right to ask such a question."

Gaines looked at the traveler, and as was the case with the sheriff, the more the two spoke, the more the captain became convinced that this was, indeed, Aaron Burr.

Gaines finally announced, "I arrest you at the instance of the federal government."

Burr calmly replied, "You are a young man and may not be aware of the responsibilities which result from arresting travelers on private business."

"I am aware of the responsibilities," Gaines said. "But I know my duty."

And with that, Burr was arrested and held at Fort Stoddert, where his charm made him a popular prisoner with both the soldiers and settlers. He played chess with Judge Toulmin's daughter. He even gave aid to Gaines when he became severely ill with stomach pains.

In recounting the story of Captain Gaines's ailment from his book *Scenes and Settlers of Mobile*, Paul Ravesies states that the encounter between Burr and Gaines was quite different, as recalled by the captain himself. Gaines noted that it was the soldiers who first arrested Burr and that he didn't meet the man until his severe bout of colic. According to Ravesies, Gaines said that Burr walked into his room with a vial to help ease the captain's pain and said, "I am Aaron Burr and a prisoner here, captured yesterday while going to Mobile. As soon as I can have a hearing, the infamous charges trumped up against me will fail. In the meantime, while compelled to remain within these walls, let us try to make our time pass as pleasantly as possible."

One month later, Burr was floated up the Alabama River to Lake Tensaw, where he was turned over to federal authorities and tried for treason.

Burr went to trial in August, but the prosecution could not find a single witness to prove that he had committed treason against the country. And with that, on September 1, Burr was acquitted and set free. Mobile and the western Spanish territory of Florida never became an independent country but soon after became part of the United States.

6

ROGUES OF THE SEA

B ordered by a rim of snowy white beaches, the turquoise waters of the Gulf of Mexico bring to mind the quintessential setting for swashbuckling pirates, and indeed, there were pirates and privateers that roamed these waters from Pensacola to New Orleans, making stops—or their home base—in Mobile. A few of those tales of pirate plunder come from what has been called the Golden Age of Piracy, which fell between the years 1650 and 1720. And yes, Mobile had its own share of pirates, not only during that seventy-year period but into the early 1800s as well.

The first recorded pirate to visit Mobile was former slave Laurens de Graaf. De Graaf was a mulatto (a person with mixed race origins) and a native of the Netherlands. He was captured and enslaved by Spain and sent to work on a plantation in the Canary Islands.

De Graaf was able to free himself when he found an opportunity to escape from a ship that was transferring him to another Caribbean plantation. Two years later, de Graaf met up with a group of Spanish pirates, and together they attacked a Spanish settlement in Campeche, Mexico, where he absconded with his own ship and 120,000 silver pieces. From there, de Graaf began amassing quite a fortune as a pirate, raiding any Spanish shipping he could reach in the Gulf of Mexico, and was soon labeled the "Scourge of the Spanish Main."

The pirate had a female consort, Anne Dieu-le-Veut, whom he met and married under strange circumstances. Dieu-le-Veut was a French criminal who was sent to serve time in the penal colony of Tortuga. There she married a swashbuckler by the name of Pierre Lelong. It is unclear how the couple left Tortuga, but six years later, they were in a bar when they met up with de Graaf. Lelong and de Graaf somehow found themselves embroiled in a bar fight, with Lelong coming up on the short end of the deal, dying by the hands of the other.

Dieu-le-Veut was so distraught at the death of her husband, she challenged de Graaf to a duel to avenge his death. But instead of taking up a sword, de Graaf was filled with admiration for the young woman's courage and asked for her hand in marriage. She accepted, and the two sailed off on a career of wedded piracy.

In 1699, as Pierre Le Moyne d'Iberville voyaged to the northern Gulf of Mexico where he and his brother would establish the first settlement that would become Mobile, the ship they were sailing on was refused entry into the port of Pensacola, which was under Spanish control. The reason, at least in part, was because the pilot that d'Iberville had contracted with to guide his ship through Gulf waters was none other than Laurens de Graaf. By this time, De Graaf had ended his pirating ways and was working with the French government in their exploration of the northern Gulf Coast. Since he was wanted by the Spanish government, the ship was refused entry and forced to sail on.

After leading d'Iberville to Biloxi and Mobile, it is believed that de Graaf returned to Saint Dominique, but from there, his fortunes are unclear.

The first known pirate raid in the Mobile area came on September 9, 1711, when a French brigantine appeared off the coast of Dauphin Island (then known as Massacre Island), which was under French control. The ship appeared to be in distress, so locals rushed to aid their countrymen only to be surprised when they were taken hostage. As it turns out, the ship was not French but a British corsair. It was crewed by privateers—pirates employed by a government.

Confusion reigned on the island, and the British were able to easily capture it without firing a shot. Over three days, they ransacked the island's warehouses, burned most of the settlement to the ground and tortured some residents to find out if they were hiding anything else of value.

But the islanders were not defeated. As the British privateers returned once again to continue their pillaging, the islanders began firing what guns they had left at the marauders. After firing a few rounds, they would dash from that location to another and begin firing again. Then they would stop firing, move to another location and fire again. With all of this gunfire coming from different positions, the British thought that troops had arrived from Fort Louis de la Louisiane and the privateers fled the scene.

One of the most famous pirates of the Gulf also paid a visit to the Mobile area, the "Gentleman Pirate of New Orleans," Jean Lafitte.

Lafitte was a unique character and a jack of all trades. He was not only a pirate but also a smuggler, a slave trader and a patriot acting as a privateer during the War of 1812 with Andrew Jackson during the Battle of New Orleans in exchange for a pardon.

Historians continue to debate whether or not Lafitte built an artillery battery just south of Mobile in what is now known as Bayou La Batre. Whether or not he did is a moot point because the town's people believed it. Upon hearing that Lafitte might be in their neck of the woods, locals in the quiet fishing village began sprinkling holy water over their doorways, believing it would protect them from Lafitte and his crew. Parents instilled fear in their children with stories of how Lafitte could reach out of the waters of the gulf and bayou and drag them away after the sun went down.

To be a pirate, you had to be part robber and part con man with plenty of charisma and character. That description fit J.J. Mitchell to a T. The pirate eventually made his home in Mobile as a sailmaker but began his pirating career from his home base in Cuba.

With only one eye, a weather-beaten face, billowing white trousers, a short jacket with anchor buttons and the quintessential pirate Havana hat, Mitchell certainly looked the part. He was a skillful seaman and was able to command his eighteen-man crew to maneuver his barge stealthily out of the range of his target's cannons then swiftly move in for the kill, rowing directly alongside the target vessel to board it and take its wares.

Mitchell was noted as being gentlemanly and a man of honor. Case in point: Word reached Mitchell that a ship out of Jamaica was sailing with ten thousand silver coins on board. Mitchell wheeled his barge up to the ship, boarded it and had a glass of wine with the captain before removing all of the loot. In return, Mitchell gave the captain a receipt.

The pirate and his lieutenant decided that the crew didn't need to share the loot, so they put the men ashore on an island for a little rest and relaxation, then sailed off for New Orleans with their pockets full of silver coins and the men left stranded on the island.

Upon the pirates' arrival in the Crescent City, police immediately became suspicious of the two strangers, and the chase was on. Mitchell holed up in the Louisiana swamps for a time before making his way to Mobile, where he took on the persona of a well-respected sailmaker and married a Port City woman. It didn't take long, however, for rumors to begin spreading about his plundering past. The rumors ran rampant through the city, eventually driving him out of town. When the *Mobile Commercial Register* wrote a piece chronicling his life as a pirate, Mitchell shot back, "It is false, totally false, that I ever was a pirate, and I defy any and every one of my accusers to furnish the smallest degree of evidence in support of the charge."

And that was the last we heard from J.J. Mitchell.

At about the same time, headlines were blaring with word of yet another pirate, one that would be called the "peskiest" of them all to ply the waters in and around Mobile. He was known by many aliases—Hugh Glass, John Scott, John Carney. His real name was Patrick "Paddy" Scott, and for twenty years, Paddy evaded the grasp of the law to raid shipping along the northern Gulf. He was captured several times but always managed to escape. Lather, rinse, repeat.

The first time the Irishman appears in newspapers is on April 18, 1818, in an advertisement placed in, of all places, a Tuscaloosa paper. Using his real name, Scott offered secure shipping of goods for merchants on his "excellent forty-ton barge." He went on to boast of his skills in navigating the winding Alabama waterways.

Was it an honest, aboveboard business opportunity for Scott? No one knows, because the next time we hear from Paddy is in May 1824, when, along with ten Spanish sailors in a stolen launch, he boarded the British schooner *Tar*, which was anchored in Mobile Bay, and demanded all of the goods, food and liquor. Later that same year, Scott raided the Colombian privateer *Centilla*, which was anchored in the Mobile River. His crew made off with what was described as quite a haul of dry goods and "other items of value."

The *New York National Advocate* printed a warning to all who sailed the northern gulf, suggesting that the public would "do well to be on their guard" against this band of pirates. The mayor of Mobile offered up a fifty-dollar reward for Scott's capture.

That same year, an inspector for the Port of Mobile visited Pascagoula Bay, where he discovered a bounty of goods stolen from the schooner *Barbarete*. The suspects were Paddy Scott and his crew. Authorities were able to arrest Scott and his men and lock them up in the Mobile jail, but their stay didn't last long. One of Scott's men, simply known as "Smiley," was able to saw his manacles off, wrest the keys from a jailer after knocking him down and release Scott from his cell—just that easy, the men were off again to continue where they had left off.

Scott and his band of pirates were known as "brown water" pirates. Instead of plying the blue-green waters of the Gulf of Mexico, they preferred to cruise the inland waters of bays and their many backwater channels where ships would anchor up for a night or two and would be more difficult to catch on the fly in their quick schooner, the *John Fowler*.

But the pirates would venture out into the gulf from time to time, and one day, Scott's schooner was spotted by the new Revenue Marine Service (the precursor of the U.S. Coast Guard) just off of Horn Island. Mobile newspapers announced:

> *A man named Paddy Scott has been arrested and imprisoned with a man named Smilie [sic]. He was captured off Horn Island in a small sloop by Captain Foster of the revenue cutter. Six shots were fired at him before he surrendered. Scott has long been accused of piracy and is said to be a desperate fellow.*

Realizing that the Mobile jail wouldn't hold Scott, authorities sent him literally up the river—the Mobile and Alabama Rivers—to a prison at Cahawba near Selma, but once again, it wasn't long before the jail would be missing a few prisoners. Scott and four of his crew escaped and headed back to Mobile to continue their plundering.

By 1826, the name Paddy Scott was known from New Orleans to Pensacola as he and his accomplices raided shipping almost at will, prompting the *Pensacola Gazette* to write, "Is there not promptness enough in the country to take such measures as will lead to the capture of so vile a pirate as he is known to be? Or shall we suffer him to go at large, to and fro, seeking whom he may devour?"

Occasionally, small articles appeared in the local newspapers about Scott and his whereabouts. Sometimes, he would work by himself, as was the case in early 1832 when a group of people visiting the area from Charleston hired Scott to take them from Bay St. Louis to Biloxi on a schooner. They had no clue who they were dealing with. During the journey, the travelers asked if they could stop at an island to do some hunting. Scott obliged, and when the visitors disembarked, he turned the boat around and sailed away—leaving them ashore and taking all of their belongings.

And not all of Scott's "jobs" were on the water. In late 1832, Scott and his men landed on the Eastern Shore of Mobile Bay, where they stole cattle and terrorized residents. His actions were called "vile outrages" by the press. In response, Mobile, New Orleans and Pensacola created a dragnet—a coordinated land and sea search for the pirate and his men. A $500 reward was offered.

Scott was brazen in his taunting of the law. He would openly walk down the streets of New Orleans, for example, and wouldn't be noticed or questioned—that is, until word came through the *New Orleans Courier*: "It appears that he [pirate Paddy Scott] arrived in this city, four or five days ago, from Mobile, and was arrested last night near the levee in the first municipality."

New Orleans police finally apprehended Scott on a charge of vagrancy. Unfortunately, the slippery Scott was released once again, this time because there was not enough evidence to pin the Eastern Shore crimes on him.

The end of Paddy Scott's pirating career came in 1840, when he stabbed James Burgoyne in the back in New Orleans then fled to Mobile. Scott was immediately arrested upon his arrival in the Port City and extradited to New Orleans to stand trial for murder. Onlookers in the courthouse were quoted as saying that he looked like an "idiotic, mindless looking man and apparently devoid of all physical courage."

Scott was sentenced to death by hanging, but the jury took pity on him and requested that the governor spare his life. The governor agreed, and Scott was set free yet again—but this time, he had learned his lesson and no longer terrorized shipping in the region. He would spend the rest of his life working as a boat pilot on Lake Ponchartrain until his death in 1844.

7

THE EGGNOG PARTY AND THE MOST BEAUTIFUL MARDI GRAS EVER

Across the country, neighboring cities have always had a good, friendly rivalry about one thing or another. For Mobile and New Orleans, the first two settlements on the central Gulf Coast, their rivalry revolves around the traditions of Mardi Gras. Who held the first balls? Who had the first mystic society? And, most importantly, who celebrated the first Mardi Gras in America?

There are a couple of things that we have to clarify before we talk about Mardi Gras. First of all, Mardi Gras is actually a single day—Fat Tuesday—the day when people let down their hair, release their inhibitions and celebrate like there's no tomorrow before the holy season of Lent begins the following day. The two-week celebration that precedes Mardi Gras Day is called Carnival. During those fourteen days, huge and ornate papier-mâché floats outfitted with masked revelers parade down the streets of Mobile and New Orleans, rocking back and forth to the rhythm of marching bands while riders throw trinkets to the thousands of onlookers on the ground who beg with outstretched hands. "Throw something to me, mister!" And they do—colorful beaded necklaces, huge stuffed animals and the most desired throw, the Moon Pie. Even though there is this distinction between Mardi Gras and Carnival, most people just refer to the entire two weeks as Mardi Gras.

By the way, those Moon Pies are a relatively new throw from a Mardi Gras float. Prior to 1950, it was common for revelers to throw boxes of Cracker Jack to the crowd. Needless to say, that was a painful catch for parade goers, so the city banned the sweet treat from parades, but the quick-thinking mystic societies came up with an alternative: the quintessential southern treat, the Moon Pie. Today, the Moon Pie is revered as a Mardi Gras and Mobile tradition. They even drop a six-hundred-pound electric replica of a Moon Pie on New Year's Eve from the RSA Trustmark Tower downtown.

Before we get into a little hidden history of Mardi Gras and Carnival, it's good to know where and how it all began. Records show that French explorer Pierre Le Moyne d'Iberville noted in his journal entry of March 3, 1699, that it was Mardi Gras Day, and that was all it said. There was no record of any celebrations. Other journal records from d'Iberville's brother, Jean Baptiste Le Moyne de Bienville, made reference to Mardi Gras in the French settlement of Fort Louis de la Louisiane in 1703, but again, there are no records of what that celebration consisted of, if there was one. All we can be sure of is that there were no parades like those staged today.

The first recognized celebration was on New Year's Eve in 1830 when Michael Kraft and a like-minded group of friends who were in "jolly spirits" passed a hardware store that is believed to have been located at the foot of Government Street between where the current-day Convention Center and Cooper Riverside Park is located. Some accounts say that the group picked up rakes and cowbells that were on display outside the store, while others say that Kraft sat down on the stoop in front of the store, knocking some rakes and cowbells to the ground. In either case, the group picked up the items and began parading down the streets of Mobile making quite a racket. When someone asked the name of the group, the quick-thinking Kraft announced, "The Cowbellion de Rakin Society!"

From that humble beginning, the tradition of Mardi Gras in America began. Six members of the Cowbellions moved to New Orleans and started the Order of Comus. Parades grew in number in both cities and switched to parading the two weeks prior to Lent. These parades were organized by groups of mysterious masked revelers who kept their identities secret, and before long, these mystic societies also began to grow in number. Mobile and New Orleans continued to regularly trade traditions back and forth.

So while Mobile is recognized as the birthplace of Mardi Gras in America (hence the nickname Mother of Mystics), it is fair to say that you can't separate Mobile and New Orleans from the history of Carnival. The celebration wouldn't be the same without either one.

As mentioned earlier, all Mardi Gras celebrations revolve around mystic societies, social organizations that are usually based on class, economic status, race or sex. Most societies operate in absolute secrecy, wearing masks and costumes to protect their identity, hence the term "mystic." More modern groups recruit members from the general public, but in either case, the waiting list to become a member is long.

The societies hold different functions throughout the year for their members but really shine during Carnival season when they organize elaborate parades with floats and throws. A king and queen are chosen to preside over the festivities, which culminate in an elaborate formal ball where the party really begins.

Mardi Gras celebrations were suspended at the outset of the Civil War and for a short period following the war during Reconstruction, a time that was meant to mend the divided nation and heal wounds. For Southerners, it was a dismal time. They were reeling from having just lost the war and were being occupied by the U.S. military, which only poured salt on the wound.

Mobile wanted to break loose from its depression and needed to celebrate. The original mystic society, the Cowbellion de Rakin, took to the streets once again on New Year's Eve 1866. The following year, five young men decided to put together a brand-new mystic society. One of the men, Harry Pillans, was looking for a fitting name for the organization. Taking inspiration from the International Order of Odd Fellows (IOOF), he came up with the name Order of Myths. Morton Toulmin designed the society's emblem. The centerpiece of the emblem is a broken column—the "column of life" —which, although there has been much speculation about this, symbolizes the broken spirit of the South after being defeated in the war. Around the column we see two figures. The first is Death, a creepy-looking skeleton with a big, bulky skull. The second is the gaily costumed figure of Folly, which represents good times and frivolity. Folly is seen chasing Death around the column, beating him with an inflated pig's bladder, signifying that on Mardi Gras, Folly defeats Death.

When the Order of Myths, or OOM, first paraded in 1868, the organization brought the emblem to life by placing a replica of the column on a mule-drawn cart. Two masked revelers—one dressed as Folly, the other as Death—ran about the column, with Folly whacking Death with a gilded pig's bladder. The cart proceeded down the street in the soft glow of flambeaux, or lighted torches. To this day, the Order of Myths' (the city's oldest surviving mystic organization) is the last parade of the season, with Folly chasing Death atop a mule-drawn cart signifying the end of Carnival.

As mentioned earlier, each mystic society hosts a gala ball following a parade where revelers remain in costume, while others dress to the nines in

An 1880 invitation to the Order of Myths' thirteenth anniversary party. *Mobile Public Library/Mobile Public Library Digital Collections.*

formal wear and party the night away. There are some society traditions, however, that take place at other times during the year, like the OOM's Eggnog Party.

It is believed that the Eggnog Party was first held by the original Cowbellion de Rakin Society. When one of the Cowbellions, Judge Joseph Seawell (who was described as an "ancient and seasoned Cowbellion") became the OOM's first president, he brought the tradition with him. The party is held annually just before Christmas to celebrate not only the holiday but also welcome new members, remember those who have passed away and raise a toast to continued fun and frolic in the upcoming year.

The party also pays tribute to past traditions and societies, in particular the old Cowbellions. For the celebration, the OOMs use a china bowl with the gilded image of the Cowbellion emblem emblazoned on it. The bowl was crafted by Ashworth Brothers of Hanley, England. No one knows for sure exactly when the bowl was created. They do know that it had to have been somewhere between 1862 when the Ashworth company first opened its doors and the end of the Cowbellion society in the 1890s.

The highlight of the Eggnog Party is the singing of the "Eggnog Song," which is sung to the tune of "Auld Lang Syne" and reprinted here so you, too, can join in:

Come, gather 'round the Eggnog bowl,
With voices strong and clear,
And sing once more that good old song,
For Christmas-tide is here.
O Christmas-tide, O Christmas-tide!
The best time of the year,
To gather 'round the bowl and sing
With voices strong and clear.

We meet fraternally to-night,
To have a Christmas cheer,
And drink our fill of good Eggnog,
For the departing year.
O Christmas-tide, O Christmas-tide!
How pleasant to be here,
Where we can fill up with Eggnog,
And speed the parting year.

To those who've joined since last we sang
Around this bowl last year,
A hearty welcome to them all,
They're all our friends most dear!
O Christmas-tide, O Christmas-tide!
With true friends gathered near,
We hail our mystic tie that binds
Us closer year by year!

We'll drink a bumper silently,
And wipe away a tear,
And think of those not here tonight
Who met with us last year.
O Christmas-tide, O Christmas-tide!
With memories so dear;
Heaven grant that all now here may meet
Around this bowl next year.

Then gather 'round the Eggnog bowl,
And sing with voices clear,
A Merry Christmas to us all
To all a Glad New Year.
O Christmas-tide, O Christmas-tide!
With memories so dear;
Heaven grant that all now here may meet
Around this bowl next year.

Inclement weather has occasionally made guest appearances during Carnival season over the years. High winds and flooding rains would try to dampen spirits but never succeeded. One story that was recorded by Palmer Pillans, the son of Harry Pillans, told of the Mardi Gras Storm of 1899.

Now keep in mind, we're talking about Mobile, Alabama, on the Gulf Coast. Even in the dead of winter, temperatures rarely dip below twenty degrees, so the storm of 1899 was a peculiarity for the Port City.

Pillans recalled that it was the day before Fat Tuesday when the temperatures began dropping. Across town, clouds rolled in, and before nightfall, four inches of snow had accumulated on the ground.

The temperatures continued to plummet, and the snow turned into sleet. At the customshouse on the corner of Royal and St. Francis Streets, the thermometers at the weather service read two degrees above zero. In the outlying suburbs, the temperatures hit four degrees below zero.

The sleet began to accumulate and coated the entire city in a two-inch-thick blanket of ice. The city ground to a halt. Nothing could move. Even railway service and the city's streetcars were out of commission.

At the Pillans home, there was no running water, so Palmer had a bowl and a pitcher in his bedroom filled with water so that he could wash up in the morning. When he awoke the next morning, the water had frozen solid in the pitcher and he had to smash the ice so he could use what water he could from it.

Palmer was in the OOM court that year and would be riding in the parade. At the time, there were no ornate floats in Carnival parades like there are today. Instead, revelers would ride decorated horses. Palmer walked over to his barn to get his horse ready for the parade but the horse couldn't move. The ice had made it impossible for the animal to get a grip on the natural skating rink that had glazed the city. Palmer and all of the other OOM riders had blacksmiths add calks to their horses' shoes. Calks are small metal projections that would stick out beneath the horseshoe and dig into the ice. You might consider them studded snow tires of the day.

Palmer said that it was so cold that he had to wear four undershirts and two pairs of long handles. Of course, Mardi Gras celebrations are known for considerable consumption of alcohol, and according to Palmer, the Order of Myths continued that tradition that frigid day. "All of us drank profusely," he said, "and nobody got lit because of the cold."

Despite the bitter cold, despite two inches of ice and four inches of snow blanketing the ground, the parade went on and everyone agreed with Palmer's summation of the day:

> *The sun came out and it was beautiful. The cold weather held and I think probably it was the most beautiful Mardi Gras Mobile has ever had because the ice and snow were everywhere and the city was brilliantly lighted and was so prettily reflected.*

8

EXCELSIOR!

In Mobile, as well as New Orleans and Pensacola, you will hear the term *Creole* used to describe a community of people of color who are descendants of French and Spanish settlers and either free or slave African Americans. In the Port City, Creole families are among the oldest, a direct link between colonial Mobile of the 1700s and present-day Mobile. Many in the community can actually trace their roots all the way back to those times when the white male settlers had children with free or slaved concubines, many of whom they freed along with their children.

Throughout the years, this close-knit community maintained its own social institutions, including schools, churches and businesses. The Creoles were known to speak a form of French that was described as being "peculiar to Mobile" all the way up into the late 1920s.

Six years after Mobile was seized from Spain, making it part of the Mississippi Territory and officially a property of the United States, the city procured its first fire engine. It was given to Jean Baptiste Trenier, who used it to organize the city's first fire company, which became known as Creole Steam Fire Company No. 1, on March 13, 1819.

Eighty men joined the brigade, and they were all needed. The engine was a simple wooden box on wheels with empty buckets onboard. The box was pulled by the men through the deep, sandy streets of Mobile to the fire. Once they arrived, they would fill the buckets at cisterns—which were few and far between—form a line and pass the buckets one at a time to the actual fire. The fire alarm was a simple metal rim off a wagon wheel that

Mobile's first fire station, Creole Fire House No. 1, was not only a fire brigade but also the birthplace of the Excelsior Band. *Author's collection.*

was suspended in the air and beaten with a hammer. At the time, there was no need for ladders or axes because every house and business already had those implements and the tallest building in the city was only two stories.

Creole Fire Company No. 1's first fire came in September of that year at Judson's Cotton Gin on Dauphin Street between Royal and Water Streets. In October, the firefighters fought another blaze at Planters Alley, but this time they found themselves surrounded by the flames and were forced to abandon the engine, which was destroyed. The engine was later replaced by a new vehicle donated by local resident James Innerarity. The firefighters' work continued.

The formation of other volunteer fire companies quickly followed, including the Neptune Engine Fire Company No. 2, but as these new white brigades were formed, the Creole station remained a separate entity away from the city fire department until 1888, when it was absorbed into the Mobile Fire Department (MFD). Company No. 1 did not disband until 1970, when MFD became integrated.

While the company was integral in saving thousands of dollars in property and many lives, the issue of getting water to a remote location to douse the flames was a real problem. In 1870, the unit was the first in Mobile to experiment with what could be considered the city's first fire hydrants.

On March 19, 1870, Creole Fire Company No. 1 drilled three wells on St. Joseph Street in downtown Mobile directly across from Bienville Square. A large crowd gathered to watch as the three wells were connected. The pumper's hoses were connected and began to suck water out of the first well. The *Mobile Weekly Tribune* reported:

> *Creole Steam Fire Co No 1 proceeded with the trial and the result was a steady stream of water with very little air intervening for half an hour. No sand was drawn up from the well for had there been, this would have been deemed reason sufficient to reject the plan. We are pleased to learn that old and experienced firemen pronounce the trial a complete success. The want of water in remote parts of the city has occasioned untold losses of property and it is a source of congratulation that the great desideratum is at last in reach of all.*

One year prior to the experiment, the company moved into a building designed and built especially for them by architect James Hutchisson. The two-story brick building was located (and still is to this day) at the corner of Dearborn and St. Francis Streets. Not only did it house the fire company's equipment, which included a horse-drawn steam pumper that was always at the ready with a load of coal in the fire box and kindling to get the steam going and water flowing, but it was also a center of activity for the Creole community, with music always the centerpiece.

One of the legendary musical groups from Mobile was spawned by the Creole Fire Company—the Excelsior Band.

John A. Pope, who was one of the early presidents of the Creole Fire Company, and his wife, Odeil, were expecting a child. To celebrate, John decided to form a band. He pulled together eighteen musicians and began practicing. The big day arrived on November 23, 1883. John and Odeil welcomed a son into the world—John C. Pope—and he was heralded in with the brass and drum rhythms of what became known as the Excelsior Band.

The band, which is still going strong to this very day, is known for its Dixieland, blues and jazz style and plays many different functions not only in Mobile but across the Gulf Coast as well, sometimes as many as three hundred events a year. What it is best known for, however, are appearances during Mardi Gras. The band first paraded during Carnival in 1884 and has never stopped. In a 1961 interview with *Sketch Magazine*, John C. Pope explained that the band used to be the last element in a Mardi Gras parade. "Because," he said, "[the] people would follow and dance behind us all over Mobile."

"Most Mobilians remember the band when it played for dances at the old Brookley Park," he said. "We played many times with the Sam Morgan and Po Celestine Brass Bands from New Orleans. We called the two-band affairs 'Double Rushes' because when one band stopped playing the other aggregation got its cue to start playing."

It's difficult to gain a spot in the band because most members never leave. Many of the players made a home with the Excelsior Band for fifty years or more or until they couldn't play anymore. Some of the band members broke out of Mobile to make a career of it, including Charles Melvin Williams, better known as famed big band trumpeter "Cootie" Williams.

Cootie was born on July 24, 1908. The nickname is said to have been bestowed on a very young Williams when his father took him to see a live concert. When his father asked him to describe the band's playing, he said, "Cootie, cootie, cootie!" He was called that ever since.

Raised by an aunt after his mother passed away, Cootie learned to play trombone, tuba and drums with his school band. then went on to teach himself the trumpet. Soon, Cootie was good enough to hook up with some

Big band trumpeter Charles "Cootie" Williams learned his chops as a member of the Excelsior Band. *William P. Gottlieb/Ira and Leonore S. Gershwin Fund Collection, Music Division, Library of Congress.*

local bands, first the Holman's Jazz Band and then the Excelsior Band. By the age of fourteen, he had moved from Mobile to Pensacola, where he played with Ross's De Luxe Syncopators. That was in 1926. The following year, the band packed up its instruments and moved to New York City, where it played local clubs and caught the ear of the legendary Duke Ellington. Ellington was having issues with one of his band's trumpet players who was battling alcoholism. Needing a replacement, he asked Cootie to join the band, and without hesitation, he did. Ellington was so impressed with the young trumpeter that in 1940 he penned a song for him, "Concerto for Cootie." The song's title was later changed to "Do Nothing Till You Hear from Me" when words were written for it.

Williams was influenced by jazz trumpeter Louis Armstrong but had a unique style of trumpet playing all his own. He could give the instrument a "growl" sound when using a mute in the bell. It was a sound that fit well with Ellington's music of the late 1930s.

From there, Cootie's career continued to soar, recording with big band notables Fletcher Henderson, Chick Webb, Billie Holiday and the "King of the Licorice Stick," Benny Goodman. After a short stint playing with several other bands and an incredible solo career, Cootie returned to Ellington's band in 1962 and stayed with him until the Duke died in 1974. Until that time, Cootie was the oldest surviving member of Ellington's original 1920s band. Williams passed away on September 15, 1985.

The Excelsior Band was only the beginning for the Mobile Creole community's musical legacy. That legacy branched out like a giant live oak tree to the far reaches of the country and the world through records, radio and even motion pictures when the granddaughters of the Excelsior Band's founder, John A. Pope, joined together to harmonize with a sound that was so unique it was hard to describe. The go-to place for all things movie related, IMDb, describes it as being a "hot, mellow, gospel, jazzy Harlem style." They were known simply as the Pope Sisters and are considered to be the first black girl singing group.

The Pope Sisters—Una (the youngest), Odile, Eoline and Inez—were the daughters of John Clement Pope and Alice Catherine Labtre. The girls had a natural talent and glamour about them that was hard to miss. Recognizing this, their father put their voices to use and had the girls sing with his own local band, promoting them as Pope's Dreamland Serenaders.

That was the beginning of the sisters' remarkable career. They quickly became widely known along the central Gulf Coast singing not only at their church—St. Peter Claver Catholic Church—but also on programs broadcast from the Battle House Hotel in downtown Mobile over WODX and from the Pensacola Saenger Theater over WCOA. They were invited to sing at parties and events thrown by Mobile's high society.

With all of this local fame, it was obvious that it was time for the girls to make a career of it. Headlines in entertainment sections of newspapers around the country sang their praise with headlines like "Pope Sisters Popularity Sweeping Southland" and "Pretty Foursome Thrills Crowds in New Orleans." There was only one way their career could go from here—up.

In the midst of the Great Depression, the girls headed to the entertainment mecca of the world, New York City. Most artists head to the big city with only dreams of making it big, praying that they might catch a lucky break. The Pope Sisters didn't need luck. They were walking headlong into stardom. Before they left the Port City in 1933, the buzz about the quartet was already reaching the Northeast. A headline in the entertainment section of the January 28, 1933 *Pittsburgh Courier* read, "Pope Sisters Are Radio's Newest Sensation: 4 Pretty Girls Female Edition of Mills Brothers?" The article then went on to talk more about the "Pride of Mobile, Alabama," reading almost like a teen magazine of the 1960s:

> *The big news of the week is the discovery of the Pope Sisters, a quartet of charming young maidens who could be compared to the identical prototype of the famed Mills Brothers.…It is indeed unusual and surprising to find a lovely family possessed of a bevy of talented and ambitious young women, entrancingly beautiful, exceedingly attractive with such effervescent personality ideals.*

> *Odile M. Pope, the eldest sister: Graduated from the Heart of Mary High School in 1928 and attended Xavier College. Plays a fine game of tennis. Eoline D. Pope: pursued a business course and is a stenographer for her father in [his] undertaking establishment. Her hobby is horseback riding. Inez O. Pope is a clever little dancer and she and her sister Una make a snappy team. Dark brown hair and brown eyes and creamy complexion. Una F. Pope is the baby of the family [and] is just sweet 16. She is crazy about Cab Calloway…Is very much interested in her father's undertaking business. A dainty little miss with dimples 'n' everything.*

After the sisters arrived in New York, their career began the preverbal meteoric rise. The girls were signed to sing at the Lafayette Theater and were a smash hit. From there, the quartet began expanding its fan base, playing elite clubs throughout the city. One headline read "Harlem Awaits Debut of the Pope Sisters," and once again, they wowed the crowd.

The Pope Sisters began touring throughout the Northeast and Canada before signing contracts to perform on several nationally syndicated NBC radio shows. They even appeared onstage with Duke Ellington.

And then came the movies. They signed on to do singing roles in two feature movies directed by pioneer black filmmaker Oscar Micheaux—the 1935 film *Temptation* and 1937's *Underworld*. Both movies dealt with the gangster world in Harlem. The sisters' credits in the movies simply read "Pope Sisters—Singers."

Mobile's Creole community produced many musical talents like the Treniers, who rocked the world in the 1940s and '50s. *Public domain.*

They also appeared in several shorts in 1935, including *The Life of the Party* and *Here's the Gang*, the latter being a short that is centered on a house party where an eclectic group of performers puts on a show. Everything is thrown into the film: ballroom dancing, Russian and cowboy tunes, crazy dance steps and the Pope Sisters singing one of their, as the theater card says, "hot songs."

For a short time, the quartet became a trio when Una retired from the group in 1940 and married a longtime friend from Mobile, Martin Tuttle. It wasn't long after that this short but sweet ride to stardom came to an end. The youngest of the group—Una—was the last to pass away in 2009 at the age of 102.

One more Creole group from Mobile made its mark on the music world and deserves mention here, the Treniers.

The band was assembled in 1947 with Milt, Claude, Cliff and Buddy Trenier along with Eugene Gilbeaux, Henry Tucker Green on drums and Don Hill. The Treniers played not only R&B but also a form of what has been called "jump blues," a blend of swing music and blues. Their performances were electric, with the band doing high jumps and crazy little dance steps.

While the band's sound was influenced by the music of Jimmie Lunceford's big band, especially his hit song, "Rhythm Is Our Business," the door swung both ways, with the band being a big influence on others, most notably, rock legend Bill Haley and the Comets, making the Treniers one of the early pioneers in the then new world of rock 'n' roll.

The band was featured in several cookie-cutter rock 'n' roll pictures of the 1950s, including *Don't Knock the Rock* in 1954 and the 1955 film *The Girl Can't Help It!*, which Paul McCartney of the Beatles said influenced some of his own songs. The movie starred Hollywood bombshell Jane Mansfield and featured appearances by Fats Domino, Little Richard, the Platters and the Treniers singing "Rockin' on Sunday."

The Treniers recorded six albums and dozens of singles, toured England and appeared on television with Jerry Lewis and Dean Martin on *The Colgate Comedy Hour* in 1954.

9

A Change of Status

One of the most intriguing and tragic pieces of hidden Mobile history came my way through a casual conversation with a friend who enjoyed digging into history. She mentioned that at one time, free people of color would petition the courts to become slaves.

Wait, what? Granted, the life of freemen was fraught with its own perils and the definition of "freeman" was loose, to say the least. The difference between the word and its actual practice could be very different. But even still, for someone to give up what all mankind craves—freedom, no matter how much or how little they actually had—to enter a life of servitude? That would seem contrary to basic human instincts.

I needed to check this out, so I traveled to the Mobile Public Library's Local History and Genealogy building. I asked the staff about these petitions and waited patiently as they looked for any information on them. I was really expecting to find only a couple of anecdotes on the subject but totally caught off guard as they directed me to a reel of microfilm. On this reel were hundreds and hundreds of petitions submitted by free people of color to the Mobile probate judge asking to become slaves.

As I skimmed through the petitions, I read many different stories, but many of them had one thing in common—fear. A fear that their way of life, and in some cases their lives themselves, were being threatened. Still others had indication as to their motive for the request.

For instance, in one petition, a young woman requested the change of status due to the fact that her husband had passed away, and since that

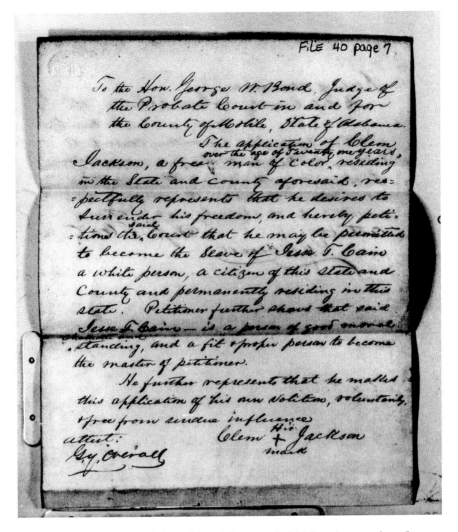

It's hard to believe, but free blacks petitioned the courts in Mobile to become slaves for various reasons. *Mobile Public Library Local History & Genealogy.*

time, she had been working as a servant for a wealthy doctor. She was on her own with no family. In her petition, she stated that after "mature deliberation on her part" and "uninfluenced by any person," she felt that her condition in life would be better because she was presently "destitute and without protection" and as a slave, she would be cared for and protected. Another, a petition submitted by twenty-one-year-old Clem Jackson, gave no clues as to his reasoning behind the request. The petition simply asked for permission to become the slave of Jesse T. Cain, a "person of good moral standing and a fit and proper person to become the master of the petitioner." The document, like most, ends with the petitioner's name written by the attorney who drafted the document and signed by the petitioner with a simple letter—X.

Quite a turnabout in the common narrative of slavery.

But that was the fear and anxiety free people of color were facing. As in the history of Reverend Shandy Jones, recounted later in this book, as the Civil War neared, many whites and white slave holders feared free blacks. In 1860, the census reported eight hundred free people of color lived in the city; plus, as a report from the Mobile Police Department stated, over one thousand slaves lived in the city apart from their masters.

Across the state, many freedmen owned and operated their own barbershops. In fact, in Mobile, over half of the shops were operated by free men of color. Whites were under the misguided impression that these businessmen would meet in the barbershops to discuss ways of causing an insurrection among slaves, then spread their message to area slaves at Sunday church services in the hopes of causing a revolt against their owners.

Nothing, of course, was further from the truth, but the feeling among free black men and women was that they were trapped. Yes, they had a reasonable amount of freedom, but now that freedom was being threatened to the point that even their lives were in danger.

Because of the fear running rampant through the white population, several proposals were made to have the Alabama state legislature write laws whereby free blacks would be required to either leave the state altogether—preferably to their own country in Liberia—or they would be sold into servitude by the state.

Nothing ever came of the proposal, but strict laws were handed down, making life increasingly difficult for the free black population. For example, several Alabama cities, Mobile included, levied excessive taxes on free blacks. Some cities established curfews to keep them off the streets at night unless a special pass was granted by the mayor.

Several freemen submitted petitions to the Mobile probate office in 1860, and by February 1861, the number of petitions being considered by the court had grown considerably, which caused the state legislature to formalize the rules for petitioning. The regulation stated that both the "master-to-be" and the free black person would be required to declare their intentions, that the petition was being submitted on the freeman's own free will and that a hearing on the matter would take place within ten days of the petition being filed.

The future master noted in the petition had some rules to follow. For example, they were not allowed to acquire the new slave and then turn around and sell him or her to someone else to pay off debts. They also had to pay the filing fee of five dollars—plus, if the person petitioning the court was under eighteen, the prospective owner would have to pay a fifteen-dollar fee for the service of an attorney who would be assigned to the case.

With emancipation, this tragic piece of Alabama and southern history came to an end. I highly recommend that readers of this book venture out to the Mobile Public Library's Local History and Genealogy building on Government Street next to the Ben May Public Library and review these records. They will leave you with a deep feeling of the desperation these people experienced, believing there to be only one way out.

10

DRESSING DOWN

From the elite aristocracy to the working class, the women of the antebellum South were demure and refined. Their demeanor was expected to demonstrate elegance and grace and the clothes they wore were designed to reflect that image.

The mid-1800s saw a new wave in women's fashion—the hourglass look with tight, almost body-busting corsets pulling the waist into literally breathtaking smallness. Both the elite and working-class women had two sets of attire, but for much different purposes.

For the elite, they would have daywear and evening wear. For daywear, just about every inch of skin was covered to avoid sunlight. At the time, it was a fashion statement to have pale white skin. It was also unseemly and highly provocative for a woman to show her neck, so collars were high, sometimes up to the chin. In those cases, the collars were removable so that they could be washed or changed for a new look.

In the evening, the prudish rules were dropped, and the women would wear voluminous skirts that billowed outward with the aid of hoops. Short sleeves exposed their arms, and the necklines were shockingly low. And in their hands, they would carry small hand purses for necessities and many times a parasol.

The same rules applied for working-class women. They, too, had two sets of clothes, but they were for much different purposes. The first set was their everyday clothes, the ones that they wore around the house to do chores or go to the market. Their evening wear, their "fancies," were nowhere near as

An example of the modest fashions of women in the antebellum South. You can understand the shock that came when Mobilians saw a woman in men's clothes on the street. *Public domain.*

elegant as the evening wear of the elite. These clothes would only be worn on special occasions, such as going to church on Sunday.

While the elite would buy material from France and England to make extravagant and fanciful gowns, the lower class settled with dresses made of fustian, osnaburg and calico in solid or striped colors.

And that's how it was for both classes of women in Mobile and throughout the South in the mid-1800s. They were expected to act and dress like women, so it wasn't a surprise when the following "shocking" news account appeared in the *Mobile Register and Advertiser* on September 12, 1861:

> *Yesterday the police arrested Ellen Bosquis, a fine, tall woman of five feet ten inches, on the charge of being in man's clothing. She had on pants that were full made and tied at the ankle, and a handsome uniform of the Confederate army. It proved that she was a vivandierie [sic] of the army, and had accompanied her regiment from New Orleans to Richmond, Va., at which place she obtained a furlough to come and see her friends in this city. Of course, she was set at liberty.*

11

UNEXPLAINED MOBILE

Towns and cities across America have their own stories of the weird and unexplained, and Mobile, with its three-hundred-plus-year-old history, is no exception. There are tales of haunted houses, mysterious occurrences and strange apparitions that warn of approaching storms.

One such tale comes from southeast of Mobile in the town of Orange Beach, Alabama, which is located directly on the Gulf Coast. Hundreds of years ago, along a stretch of land that is now part of Gulf State Park, a Native American medicine man would give a few drops of a special elixir to the warriors of his tribe before they went hunting that supposedly gave them strength and stamina. One night, one of the young warriors entered the medicine man's hut and drank an entire bottle of the elixir. The last time the young warrior was seen was as he raced into the woods with a pack of wildcats. The legend of the Catman was born.

The Catman has been seen on numerous occasions since then. During the Great Depression, a man was fishing in a pond off of Catman Road when he saw another man approach. Thinking nothing of it, he turned and continued tending to his lines. From out of nowhere, the fisherman was attacked from behind by the unknown man. Deep scratches from the "thing's" long fingernails raked the fisherman's skin, and he reported that it smelled like a wild beast. Luckily for him, a driver in a car happened to be passing by at the time of the attack and saved the fisherman.

In the 1960s, a young man was leaving his job at an A&W Root Beer stand in neighboring Gulf Shores. As he sped down Catman Road in his car, a strange-looking creature raced in front through the beam of his headlights—the Catman?

There has been much speculation over the years about what the residents of Orange Beach had seen. Some believe that the individual who attacked the fisherman may have been a homeless man who took up shelter in Gulf State Park. Still others believe it was a child who had lost his parents and home during the 1906 hurricane and was raised by wild animals. In any event, take a walk down the Catman Road Trail at Gulf State Park one evening. You may be surprised by what you see.

Back across the bay in Mobile, residents have reported the appearance of a ghostly ship on stormy nights, its sails furled in the wind, lights flickering in the intense bay breeze, only to disappear with the sound of terrified screams coming from within as it approaches landfall. It is believed that this is the French ship *Saint Louis*, which met its doom along these shores in the early 1700s.

As the story goes, the ship was carrying a group of young women, Cassette or Casket Girls, to Fort Louis de la Louisiane to marry some of the settlers in the fort. The captain of the ship was not familiar with the waters in and around Mobile Bay that led to the fort from the Gulf of Mexico, but even still, in complete darkness, he made the decision to take the ship in.

Slowly and cautiously, the captain sailed the ship into the bay; suddenly, there was a jolt that rocked the ship. The women were terrified that the ship was going to sink, but the crew reassured them that they had landed on a sand bar and ushered them back to their bunks. The captain decided that it was too risky to continue on and that they would have to wait until morning for the tide to turn and ease them off the bar.

From out of nowhere, at 1:00 a.m., lightning coursed the sky and thunder roared, echoing up and down the waterway. The captain ordered his crew to secure the ship for a great storm. As they did, he shouted, "Stranded on a sand bar and a tropical hurricane about to burst upon us in all of its fury. God deliver us!"

The storm arrived with incredible winds slamming into the ship. The vessel lurched and heaved as the bay waters rapidly rose, lifting the ship off the sand bar and propelling it with a mighty crash into the banks of the bay. The ship splintered into pieces, leaving debris and the bodies of the dead on the beach.

The following morning, local Indians found the wreckage and helped tend to the wounded. What few survivors there were made it to the fort, where they died within a few days of their arrival, all except the captain, who had to live with this tragic event the rest of his life.

Since then, when a storm is approaching from the gulf, residents say that if you look out into the bay you will hear screams of terror and see the French ship *Saint Louis* disappear into legend.

In the city itself, even more strange happenings have been reported, two of which occurred at the city's second-oldest graveyard, Church Street Cemetery. Mobile's first cemetery, Campo Santo, was relocated to this location in 1819.

The cemetery is relatively small, only four acres in size, but within the confining walls made of old Mobile brick lie some of the city's earliest residents, dignitaries and history makers like treasurer to the king of Spain Don Miguel Eslava and the man credited with bringing Mardi Gras back to the Port City after the Civil War, Joe Cain.

Visitors to the cemetery today see only remnants of its former beauty. The once beautiful granite and marble tombstones are now weathered, cracked and broken from centuries of hurricanes and, sadly, vandalism. Many of the inscriptions have long since eroded away with time and weather. Low-lying vaults with flat, solid stone tops have long since caved in. At one time, taller vaults where the bodies of up to four individuals were laid to rest graced the yard but are no longer visible today. And what was said to have been the

The site of some of Mobile's unexplained occurrences, the city's second-oldest cemetery, Church Street, that was established in 1819. *Author's collection.*

most impressive vault of them all, the "Mother Hubbard" vault, has also been reclaimed by nature.

The Mother Hubbard vault had steps that led slightly underground to an area where shelves lined the walls and the coffins of the dead were placed. According to a story told by historian Jay Higginbotham, an old woman used to pay a nightly visit to the vault, walking down the stairs carrying food and an oil lamp, and she would stay for a few days before reemerging. Everyone in town believed that she was in mourning for one of the people entombed in the vault.

A Mobile police officer who worked on the side as a night watchman saw the woman enter the vault on many occasions and would watch for her to come back out. One night, however, she never came out. The officer became concerned and walked up to the door of the vault to check on her. When he peeked inside, all he saw was the oil lamp. It flickered softly as the oil in its base began to run out. The woman had disappeared.

But one of the strangest stories from the Port City's past and another that occurred at the Church Street Cemetery is the story of Charles R.S. Boyington.

In 1833, Mobile was in the midst of rapid economic growth. Business was booming along the waterfront, and the population was growing exponentially as people began flocking in to cash in on the boon. One of those was twenty-three-year-old Charles Boyington, a printer from Connecticut.

Many of those who moved to the city found accommodations in area boardinghouses, which is what Boyington did, sharing a room with another printer, Nathanial Frost. Printers didn't make much money, but they did earn enough to get by. That didn't satisfy Boyington, who wanted something more and began to finagle his way into swanky parties, weekly affairs with Mobile's upper crust. At one of those parties, he met a young woman named Rose.

The pair fell in love, but her father would have nothing of it, saying that Boyington wasn't making the kind of money needed to properly support his daughter. He forbade Boyington from seeing his daughter ever again, but that didn't stop the young man's love for her. In fact, Boyington became more and more infatuated with the girl. He would incessantly and hopelessly write poetry to her. His infatuation became so strong that he could no longer concentrate on his job and was fired.

Now labeled an unreliable worker and in turn unable to find work, Boyington became destitute. His roommate tried to relieve some of Boyington's problems, but when Frost offered to pay Boyington's room and board until he could land a job, Boyington flew into a rage. His pride had apparently been hurt. Boyington did learn something about his roommate during the incident—Frost had more money than he let on. Would this be a motive for murder?

Frost was able to calm the situation down, but Boyington was still despondent. Frost tried to help his friend again, this time telling Boyington that he could teach the printer how to whittle beautiful wooden items, possibly to sell or perhaps to give to Rose that would show her father that he was worthy. Boyington agreed, and the pair went to their favorite spot to sit and while away the hours with casual conversation—inside the walls of the Church Street Cemetery.

Later that night, Boyington returned to the boardinghouse and was greeted by his landlord. When asked about his roommate's whereabouts, Boyington said his friend wanted to spend some time alone in the cemetery. He then handed the landlord a package to give to Rose and booked passage on the riverboat *James Monroe*, which was leaving Mobile for Montgomery.

When Frost did not return the following morning, the landlord contacted the sheriff. He immediately went to Frost's last known whereabouts—the cemetery. There, under a pile of leaves, was the body of Nathanial Frost. He had been stabbed multiple times and robbed of between fifty and sixty dollars plus his pocket watch.

The following morning, May 12, 1834, the *Mobile Advertiser* reported the murder. The story stated that Charles Boyington was the prime suspect in the case, and a reward of $500 was offered for his apprehension. Authorities located him in Montgomery and returned him to Mobile to stand trial. The jury was virtually out on Boyington before the trial even began. The *Mobile Advertiser* began reporting that Boyington had cultivated a friendship with Frost (who, by the way, was afflicted with tuberculosis) in order to kill him "for the sake of plunder." With coverage like that, thousands of angry Mobilians greeted Boyington when he was returned to the city.

The trial began in mid-November, with the prosecution focusing its case on the fact that the pair shared a room, that the two were seen leaving together the night of the murder and that Boyington returned that night alone. Throughout the trial, Boyington proclaimed his innocence, but a lynch mob mentality ruled the day, and on November 21, 1834, the jury deliberated for one hour and fifteen minutes and found Boyington guilty of first-degree murder and recommended that he should hang for killing Nathanial Frost.

Boyington spent the next nine months behind bars, where he continued to write his poetry, some of which was published in the local newspapers.

From the gallows, convicted murderer Charles Boyington said an oak tree would grow where he was buried to prove his innocence, and it did. *Author's collection.*

It was rumored that Rose actually visited Boyington in jail a few times and never once believed that he was guilty of the crime.

His case was brought to the Alabama Supreme Court on the grounds that two members of the jury should have been disqualified. Boyington's attorney argued that one of the jurors was ineligible because he was British, while the other was heard saying during proceedings that he would hang Boyington if he could. In a vote of 2–1, the appeal was denied.

The stage was set for a dramatic scene. It was a two-mile walk from the jail cell to the gallows. The procession was led by a cart that carried the coffin in which Boyington would be buried. Behind it, the convicted prisoner walked. Thousands of angry Mobilians turned out to watch the hanging, so many that the local militia was ordered to keep the peace.

Boyington climbed the gallows, and when asked by officials overseeing the hanging if he had any last words, he replied, "Sir, I am innocent! But what can I do? When I am buried, an oak tree with a hundred roots will grow to prove my innocence."

And with that, the trap door sprung and Boyington was dead. He was buried in the cemetery's potter's field.

One year later, people walking past the grave site noticed something amazing—it was a tiny seedling sprouting from the grave. A massive live oak did, indeed, grow at his grave.

You can still see the oak tree today, standing proudly on the west side of the cemetery just outside of its walls near the AME Zion Church on St. Bayou Street at Church Street. Some say if you visit at night, you will hear whispers and maybe, just maybe, see the ghost of Charles Boyington.

12

The Unreconstructed Rebel

Augusta Evans Wilson

Many Mobilians, and even many Americans, know the story of Augusta Jane Evans Wilson, the first female author to break the $100,000 earnings barrier with her romantic, sentimental novels. What makes that extraordinary is that she did it at a young age during a time when male authors dominated the literary world and female writers were not considered to be very marketable. To make it more amazing is that her success came as the country was in the throes of the Civil War. What most people do not realize, however, is that "Miss Gusta" (as she was fondly called around Mobile) had another nickname—the "Unreconstructed Rebel," a moniker she proudly earned and wore from her propagandist writings for the Southern cause and her patriotism for the Confederacy during the Civil War.

Augusta Jane Evans was born in Columbus, Georgia, on May 8, 1835, to Matthew and Sarah Evans. Her father was a successful cotton farmer, earning enough money to build his wife and eight children a glorious mansion he called Sherwood.

Augusta was an exceptionally bright child, having what people call a photographic memory. She could vividly recall sights, sounds and events in great detail years after they occurred. This would be a trait that would serve her well in her future writing career.

With the exception of attending one private school for a very short time (she had to quit due to illness), all of her education came from her mother who, even with eight children to attend to, found ample time to educate the

The "Un-Reconstructed" Rebel, author Augusta Evans Wilson, was the first woman to earn over $100,000 as an author. *Mobile Public Library Local History & Genealogy.*

young girl. Later in life, Augusta said of her mother, "[She] is in every sense my 'Alma Mater', the one to whom I owe everything and whom I reverence more than all else on earth."

The success her family knew came to an end when Augusta was five years old. After a series of encounters with Indians on their farm, a devastating flood that the family barely survived in 1841 and the sudden and rapid decline in the price of cotton, the family was financially wiped out with their plantation and most of their belongings being sold at auction. With nothing left for them in Georgia, her father bought a Conestoga wagon, packed up the family and headed west to what was known as the "New Frontier"—Texas.

The family settled down in San Antonio, where they lived for four years. The Evans family had arrived in San Antonio not long after tensions between the United States and Mexico boiled over, resulting in the famous Battle of the Alamo. The images of that fierce battle were still fresh in the town when the Evans family arrived, and those images left a deep impression on the ten-year-old Augusta.

Times were tough for the Evans family in this frontier town, and as Augusta turned fourteen, they found themselves struggling once again to make ends meet. The specter of being poor and destitute began to haunt the young woman and continued to do so for the rest of her life. Even when she began making incredible sums of money from her writing, she would always carry a $100 bill with her—just in case.

Once again, the Evans family packed up, this time heading east and settling in Mobile. Her father made an adequate salary in the Port City, enough that he was invited to become a member of the city's premier Mardi Gras society, the Cowbellian de Rakin.

Even though she was far removed from San Antonio, Augusta could not forget the images she saw and the stories she had heard in San Antonio about the Alamo. They were so vivid that she was compelled to put them to paper. She began writing the manuscript in complete secrecy, keeping it totally hidden from her family until Christmas Day 1854, when, at the age of fifteen, she presented it to her father as a present. The manuscript was titled *Inez: A Tale of the Alamo*.

With financial backing from Augusta's uncle, Augustus Howard, the manuscript was sent to Harper Publishing in New York City. The publisher agreed to put it into print. Almost immediately, the reviews came in, and they were not pretty. Most critics described the book as being just "a bad novel," pointing out that the author had not been exposed to enough literature and that the text was virtually plotless. She was also criticized for espousing a deep anti-Catholic sentiment throughout the book. For a young woman who believed in Victorian ideals, this was quite a stance to take. But that's the yin and yang of Augusta Evans. While women were trying to gain the right to vote, she believed that women should stay out of politics, saying, "The true rule is, a true wife in her husband's house is his servant; it is in his heart that she is queen." But here she was, stepping right into the thick of things, sharing some of her beliefs, which would gain her notoriety in the years to come.

It goes without saying that the book was not a huge success. At this point, many authors would have turned and walked away never to write again, but Augusta was determined. After the release of *Inez*, her writing would take a turn and become more political as she became more and more enamored of the Southern cause.

In 1859, a series of four unsigned letters appeared in the *Mobile Advertiser* that readers of Augusta's work all agree were written by her. In the letters, she did not defend the South or its institution of slavery but instead went on an attack against the North and its literary world—its writers, authors and journalists—stating that the lies that Northern publishers and newspapers spewed daily in the name of the all-mighty dollar was the real immorality in the country. In the first letter, she said that only worrying about making a buck was "a disgrace to [the] authors and insulting to the intelligence of the American people."

Her ideals about the North and South were coming into sharp focus as her pro-Southern propagandist letter writing continued. In one letter, she lists the differences between the North and South quite succinctly: The South is genial and idealistic while the North is cold and indifferent; the South is refined while the North only has a love of money that corrupts; Southern writers write from the heart with beauty while Northern writers are only commercial product; and Southerners cherish their culture and nonpartisan values of literature while the North debases literature for political gains.

That same year, the eighteen-year-old Augusta finished writing her second novel, *Beulah*, the story of an orphan who becomes the ward of a wealthy doctor who eventually falls in love with her. The story revolves around the girl's fight with spiritual skepticism, a subject she touched on earlier in the book *Inez*.

She submitted the manuscript to Appleton Publishing, which immediately rejected it. Undaunted, she resubmitted it, this time taking it in person along with her cousin, John Jones, to Derby and Jackson Publishing in New York City. As the story goes, J.C. Derby took the manuscript and brought it home for his family to read. They were enthralled with the tale and told him to publish it right away. He did, in 1859, and it sold over twenty thousand copies in nine months. The royalties from the book were enough that Augusta could purchase her family a new home on Springhill Avenue that they called the Georgia Cottage.

Love came into Augusta's life that same year when a young journalist, James Reed Spaulding, met the author while she was in New York. The two fell in love, and Augusta agreed to allow Spaulding to come to Mobile and meet her parents. Soon after, they were engaged to be married. They made an odd couple, with Augusta staunchly supporting the South, while Spaulding believed in the Union and Lincoln.

As it turns out, the letters that were published earlier that year were just the beginning of the author's propagandist writings. From those letters, she went on to attack any Southern author who opposed secession, even breaking ties with a close friend of hers, author Marion Harland, for refusing to leave her

Yankee husband and continuing to live "among the oppressors of the only free people left upon the American continent."

With war imminent and with Augusta and Spaulding's stubbornly fanatical devotion to their causes, it was inevitable that the relationship between the two would end, and indeed, it did. Immediately after secession, they broke off their engagement.

Augusta's devotion to the South only intensified. She became friends with many Confederate statesmen and generals. She was honored with a tea party thrown in her honor in Montgomery while Jefferson Davis was forming his new cabinet. Alabama state legislator Jabez Lamar Monroe Curry was known to have changed a few of his speeches based on suggestions made by Augusta. And when she wrote to General Beauregard about her upcoming novel, he took time out from his duties on the battlefield to write her a full and complete report of the battles of Bull Run and Manassas, which she would later include in her third book.

Her Southern patriotism was not only political in nature, however. She had deep compassion for the soldiers who were fighting the battles. A camp was set up near her home on Springhill Avenue that would take care of sick and injured soldiers. It was named Camp Beulah in honor of her book. She became a nurse and pitched in to help not only at Camp Beulah but also at Fort Morgan just south of Mobile on the Alabama Gulf Coast and Chickamauga near Atlanta. Augusta tended to the men's wounds and brightened their spirits by singing to them.

With the Civil War and Southern secession as the backdrop of her life, Augusta began writing her third novel, *Macaria: Altars of Sacrifice*, in 1862. Many believe that the subtitle refers to the sacrifice she made when she broke off her engagement to Spaulding.

Needless to say, times were tough during the war years. The book, which was published by West and Johnson in 1863, was printed on brown wrapping paper. The covers were simple boards wrapped in wallpaper. Even so, the book became very popular in both the North and South, and while the subject matter was neither anti-Union nor anti-North, it was a solid piece of Southern propaganda with a heavy pro-South slant, so much so that the commander of Union forces in Tennessee, General George Henry Thomas, had copies of the book confiscated from his troops and burned.

It was later discovered that a "bootleg" copy of the book was being published by Michael Doolady in New York. Unknown to Augusta at the time, when word reached her first New York publisher and friend, J.C. Derby, that Doolady was trying to capitalize on the book with an unauthorized version, Derby decided that it was time to pay a visit to the publisher. He demanded that all royalties from this bootleg version be put into a trust for the author until the end of the war. Derby won the battle, and the publisher agreed.

When the war ended, Augusta traveled to New York to visit her old friend Derby in hopes of raising some money to help her brother Howard recover from an injury he had suffered in the war. It was a huge surprise when she learned of the sizeable amount that had been accumulated from the unauthorized copy of the book.

Her follow-up to *Beulah* was an article, "The Mutilation of the Hermae." This piece wasn't as soft as its predecessor. The author returned to her heavy rhetoric against the North, this time setting sights on the "depraved and unprincipled politicians of the North" who were mutilating the American Constitution while "the civilized world gazes in amazement at their unblushing and fanatical sacrilege. The destruction of Black Republicanism [a term used to describe Northerners and their abolitionist ways] can be achieved only through the success of the Southern Confederacy." She concluded by declaring that the South was the "bodyguard for the liberty of the Republic."

When the war ended in 1865, it was time to make amends and heal the country, but some wounds are hard to mend. Augusta was invited to attend a special dinner in her honor in New York City. The event was organized by Charles O'Connor, who invited renowned authors and journalists from across the country to the event, one of those being Henry J. Raymond, the editor of the *New York Times*. Augusta refused to meet with him because of his "attitude" during the war.

Now a wealthy author, Augusta set out on a new mission. She began to raise funds to bring the bodies of soldiers who had died in the war and hailed from Mobile back home to their city to rest in peace. A section of Magnolia Cemetery on Virginia Street, the third-oldest cemetery in Mobile, was set aside for just that purpose. A tall statue of a Confederate soldier bowing his head was erected in the center of the Confederate Rest. In 1931, the statue was struck by lightning, destroying most of the figure's body. The torso and head of the monument were spared and sit on a pedestal near the original pedestal to this very day.

In 1868, Augusta married widower Lorenzo Madison Wilson. Wilson, known to all as the "Colonel," was a successful grocery store owner with four children. He was twenty-seven years older than Augusta, but that didn't matter. It was a deep romance that lasted until his death in 1892.

Prior to her own death, Augusta seemed to have a softening heart toward the North, or at least the women of the North. A close friend presented her with a book that was dedicated to the women of both the North and South. Augusta looked at it and said, "Ah, well. The women of the North as well as of the South are good and true."

In all, Augusta wrote nine novels before her death in 1909, including her most popular, the 1866 *St. Elmo*, which sold over forty million copies in four months.

The author's funeral was quite the occasion in the Port City. Newspaper accounts reported that a procession of thirty carriages carried her body to Magnolia Cemetery. Lines of cars filled with people followed the procession, and several hundred Mobilians were waiting graveside for the entourage to arrive. When the final prayers were read and Augusta laid to rest, those in attendance refused to leave, and the gates of the cemetery had to remain open way past closing time.

It was a fitting tribute to the woman who broke the barrier for female writers around the world, a woman dedicated to her cause, the "Unreconstructed Rebel"—Miss Gusta.

13

THEY TOOK MATTERS INTO THEIR OWN HANDS

The Bread Riot of 1863

Y ou can still see an image of Mobile as it looked during its antebellum past as you approach historic Oakleigh Mansion along Oakleigh Place. It's a picture postcard of the time—row upon row of majestic oaks draped in flowing, green Spanish moss. Flowering white and fragrant magnolia trees brighten the path. As you near the mansion, you see Creole cottages and then, the Victorian-era mansion itself with its elegant furnishings and spiral staircases.

Oakleigh is a throwback to a period of time from just after the War of 1812 to just before the Civil War in the South. In fact, antebellum is a Latin term—*ante bellum*—that literally means "before the war."

The antebellum years were a time when "cotton was king" in the South, making plantation owners incredibly wealthy. And while cotton was not the main farm crop in Mobile, it still played an important role in its economy, as the commodity was shipped down the Mobile and Tensaw Rivers from the Black Belt area of Montgomery and Selma to the Port City for shipment to neighboring states and countries.

All of this wealth led to luxurious lifestyles for the plantation owners and shippers and a mediocre existence at best for the workers who were just happy to have steady work. Those people included not only whites but free blacks as well and, of course, slave labor that had little hope of prospering from the boom.

It was a time when great inventions helped the economy along like Eli Whitney's cotton gin, the steam-powered printing press and the building of canals and railroads.

The city of Mobile prospered during these years and was on the move. Its population skyrocketed from a mere 3,194 residents in 1830 to 29,258 by 1860. That boom would soon put a severe strain on the city, as the affluent antebellum and "cotton is king" days came to an abrupt end with the Southern secession from the Union.

In 1860, the fate of the nation was tenuous as Southern states braced for what they believed would be an attempt by Northern states to destroy the institution of slavery. When Abraham Lincoln was elected that year, the tension boiled over, and the country was literally torn apart at the seams.

In December of that year, South Carolina voted to be the first southern state to secede from the Union. Other Southern states were quick to follow. In Mobile, the city government, with enthusiastic backing by its residents, passed a resolution that called for the immediate withdrawal of the state from the Union, calling Lincoln's election "a virtual overthrow of the Constitution and the equal rights of the state."

Alabama governor A.B. Moore called for a special state constitutional convention and on January 7, 1861, by a vote of 61–39, the motion for the state to secede from the Union passed. A new flag flew over the state capitol with only one star, signifying that the state was standing on its own and was no longer a part of the United States.

Being Alabama's only port city with access to the Gulf of Mexico, Mobile was a major hub for shipping not only cotton but many other U.S. exports as well, but this fact also made the city an immediate target of the Union navy. Almost as soon as the state seceded from the Union, Mobile faced a naval blockade. The Union navy sought to put a stranglehold on the city, cutting off all of the supplies residents desperately needed to survive that were, until that moment, shipped in from adjacent cities and states.

By late 1861, the blockade was already putting a squeeze on the city's burgeoning population. Food and clothing shortages became more prevalent. An October 1861 article in the *Mobile Register and Advertiser* newspaper went as far to tell readers how to make "An Excellent Substitute for Coffee":

For a family of seven or eight persons, take a pint of well toasted corn meal, and add to it as much water as an ordinary sized coffee-pot will hold, and then boil it well. We have tried this toasted meal coffee, and prefer it to Java or Rio, inasmuch as genuine coffee does not suit our digestive organs, and we have not used it for years. Many persons cannot drink coffee with impunity, and we advise all such to try our recipe. They will find it more nutritious than coffee and quite as palatable.

But Mobile wasn't the only Southern city suffering. Similar shortages were occurring throughout the South, with women and children suffering the most. Farms began to lay fallow as the men went off to fight the war, leaving the women unable to maintain them and grow crops. Many of these women abandoned the farms and moved to cities with the hope of finding paying jobs.

By 1863, the situation in many cities was dire. On April 2, in the city of Richmond, Virginia, over one thousand women marched through the streets. A visitor to the city, John B. Jones, wrote in his diary:

> *Not knowing the meaning of such a procession, I asked a pale boy where they were going. A young woman, seemingly emaciated, but yet with a smile, answered that they were going to find something to eat. I could not, for the life of me, refrain from expressing the hope that they might be successful; and I remarked they were going in the right direction to find plenty in the hands of the extortioners.*

The throng then moved through the city going store to store, where "they proceeded to empty them of their contents" and didn't leave until they had carts full of flour, meal, clothing and the staples needed to survive.

Back in Mobile, it wasn't only the blockade that was causing shortages. The commander of Confederate troops in Mississippi, Colonel John Pemberton, prohibited the export of corn out of the state in order to conserve the supply for his troops and Mississippi's own population, effectively cutting Mobile off.

And to exacerbate the problem, inflation on what goods Mobilians could get was running rampant. In 1862, the price of commodities skyrocketed 750 percent, either because of profiteering or individuals stockpiling goods. A pound of butter rose to $3.50, while a barrel of flour went from $44.00 to $400.00. The city even ran out of oil for the streetlamps and resorted to refilling them with pitch and hard pine knots.

By the fall of 1863, the women of Mobile, much like those in Richmond, were reaching their breaking point. One soldier's wife wrote a letter to the local newspaper, the *Mobile Register*, offering a suggestion:

> *We would make it convenient to close the doors of these extortioners in goods as well as everything else; the blockade goods do a poor man's family no good whatever. They have not enough money to buy a yard, to say nothing of a bolt of calico, domestic, or any other kind of goods. Our good Christian dealer in*

G⁴ AND REAPING.

SOUTHERN WOMEN FEELING THE EFFECTS OF REBELLION, AND CREATING BREAD RIOTS.

Southern women take to the streets to get food and supplies for their families during the bread riot of 1863. *Library of Congress Prints and Photographs Division (wood carving),* Frank Leslie's Illustrated Newspaper, *May 23, 1863.*

cloth cannot take the trouble to cut a bolt, he is losing too much money and time. I will be glad, Mr. Editor, for you to tell me who can wear these men's goods, save the families of their brother speculators. This thing has to stop.

That same week, Mobile mayor R.H. Slough wrote a letter that appeared in the paper that was directed at the richest in the city:

In order to relieve the distress which is known to exist in Mobile, the undersigned would again make an appeal to the citizens. Much has been accomplished by means of the Free Market, but much remains to be done, and I think I may with confidence expect that the charitable and Christian spirit of our people will be untiring in its efforts to furnish relief where it may be needed among the worthy and industrious. It is not necessary to give instances. They are known to the actively benevolent of the public. All that I can do is to point the way by which the end may be attained. I would suggest, therefore, that subscriptions be taken up, and that the work be prosecuted with vigor until such time as at least enough shall be done to supply the wants of those who have claims on the community and worth on the public. There are many indigent women especially who need succor. Their own wants and those of their children are calculated to touch the hardest and least sympathetic heart. Let us then, my fellow citizens, see that these worthy objects of charity are placed above the reach of absolute destitution. Money for the purpose left at my office, or at that of Capt. D. Wheeler, will be devoted to the purpose with care, so that it may reach the necessities of the most deserving.

On the morning of September 4, the women of Mobile met on Springhill Road (now Springhill Avenue). A reporter with the *New Orleans Era* described the throng as a "most formidable riot by a long-suffering and desperate population."

Some of the women were armed with banners that read "Bread or Blood" and "Bread and Peace," while others brandished hatchets, bricks and axes with every intention of breaking in and raiding the stores that lined Dauphin Street.

The Seventh Alabama Regiment of the Confederate army was dispatched to the city by General Dabney H. Maury with orders to put down the riot by any means necessary, to which the soldiers replied, "If we took any action, [we would] rather assist those starving wives, mothers, sisters and daughters of men who had been forced to fight the battles of the rebellion."

When the Seventh refused to obey Maury's orders, a parading and show regiment of cadets, the Mobile Cadets, were ordered to put down the disturbance by force. The *New Orleans Era* recalled the event as "quite a little scrimmage [which resulted] in the repulse of the gallant fellows."

The women defeated the cadets.

Left with no other choice, the recently elected mayor decided to try a peaceful negotiation with the women and promised them that if they would disperse and head back to their homes their needs and demands would be met.

Well, that worked—for a little while. The women dispersed, but later that evening they returned, this time with more anger than before and began to empty the stores of clothes, food and household goods.

It wasn't only the women who were involved in the riot. Many of the male residents not fighting the war came to their aid. The *New Orleans Era* reported one situation where even the police came to their rescue:

> *In coming down Dauphine* [sic] *Street, two women went into a Jew clothing store, in the performance of the work connected with their mission. The proprietor of the store forcibly ejected the intruders, and threw them violently down on the sidewalk. A policeman who happened to be near, thereupon set upon the Jew and gave him a severe beating.*

The women of Mobile vowed that if their suffering wasn't addressed or if the war didn't end, they would burn the city down. When all was said and done, the riots didn't end the war, and the shortages continued well into the period of Reconstruction. The women's Bread Riot of 1863 quietly came to an end.

14

THE WASHINGTON SQUARE DEER

Mobile is divided up into seven historic districts, each with its own special charm and history. One of the most popular is the Oakleigh District, where the stately Oakleigh Mansion stands, recalling the city's antebellum days. In this historic district, only two blocks south of Government Street and two blocks west of Broad Street, there is a beautiful little park—Washington Square. Along its walkways there are cast-iron castings of a small Civil War cannon. Cherubs rim the park's central fountain along with one more cast-iron statue that is a true survivor of the war, that of a deer.

The antebellum period that began in the early 1820s and ended with the outset of the Civil War spawned a renaissance in architecture that was based on either Greek or French Colonial styles. Tall houses featured large windows, sprawling balconies, grand staircases, decorative plaster work and tall porticos with decorative columns. Naturally, this style became known as antebellum architecture.

Another feature of antebellum architecture was the use of cast iron. Most balconies were lined with cast-iron railings, the portico might have cast-iron flower and plant vases welcoming guests inside and their sprawling property may have decorative cast-iron statutes of animals.

George A. Tuthill Sr. resided in one such home on Springhill Avenue. His yard was adorned with two majestic cast-iron deer, each being tended to by two cast-iron African American boys. These statues were considered the handsomest of all in the city.

A survivor of the Civil War—one of two cast-iron deer that was thrown into the Mobile River by the Union army. *Author's Collection.*

Following the Battle of Mobile Bay just south of the city at Fort Morgan and the Battle of Blakeley on Mobile Bay's eastern shore—the last major battle of the Civil War—Union troops moved across the bay and the last Confederate port city, Mobile, surrendered. Eventually, Union soldiers made their way from downtown to the Springhill area and came to the Tuthill home. The Union officer in charge of the brigade spotted the statues in the yard and took them as a challenge.

"It is an affront to our cause," he said. "Look, two Negro boys in bondage, and cast in iron at that. Free them!"

The soldiers removed the statues from the yard, and with the mission to remove all vestiges of slavery, they decided to "free" these statues from their "bondage" on the Tuthill property. The statues were unceremoniously hauled downtown to the Mobile River then thrown into the river's dark green waters.

Tuthill went into grieving, mourning the loss of his prized statues. As Union troops stationed throughout the city began to stand down, Tuthill made it his mission to find the missing artwork. He would spend thousands of dollars and an incredible number of hours trawling the river in search of the statues.

The two African American statues and one of the twin deer were never located. He was, however, able to find the other deer, and it is now standing proudly beneath the gnarled live oak branches at Washington Square.

15

FREEMAN

The Reverend Shandy Jones

While researching this book, I saw that the municipal cemeteries manager for the City of Mobile, Hereford "Tighe" Marston, would be doing a presentation on Magnolia Cemetery for a local genealogy group. Magnolia Cemetery is Mobile's third oldest. The first was the Spanish burial ground called Campo Santo.

Campo Santo was established in 1780 and was located where the current Cathedral Square can be found at the corner of Conti and South Claiborne Street directly across from the Cathedral of Immaculate Conception. The cemetery was relocated to property purchased by the city from William and Joshua Kennedy along Church Street in 1819. The Church Street property was purposely located about one half mile outside of the city limits due to fears that the bodies of those dying from a yellow fever epidemic that was ravaging the city at the time would continue perpetuating the disease. During this epidemic, well before Dr. Josiah Nott discovered the origins of the disease, almost 20 percent of the city's population died.

That yellow fever epidemic caused Church Street Cemetery to fill rapidly, and in 1867, Magnolia Cemetery was established along Virginia and South Ann Streets.

I listened intently as the speaker described the decorative hand-carved Victorian-era funerary that graces the cemetery's tombstones and mausoleums. Then he began to run through the names of some of Mobile's luminaries buried there; most were names I was familiar with—author Augusta Evans Wilson, the father of Mardi Gras Michael Kraft, one of the first African American men to be elected to the Alabama House of Representatives since 1866 and a local civil rights leader, John LeFlore. But there was one name I had never heard before—the Reverend Shandy Jones.

I spoke with Mr. Marston following the presentation, and he told me that there are literally hundreds of unmarked graves in Magnolia Cemetery, one of them belonging to Shandy Jones. He explained that up until a few years ago, not much was known about the reverend, that is until his story was unearthed by University of Alabama professor G. Ward Hubbs for his book *Searching for Freedom after the Civil War: Klansman, Carpetbagger, Scalawag, and Freedman*. As it turns out, Jones had an incredible story to tell.

Shandy Jones was born in Huntsville in 1816. Jones was the youngest of five children with two elder brothers and two sisters. Only nine days before he turned four years old, his two brothers, one of which is believed to have actually been his father, declared him a freeman of color. As a result of his mother being mulatto, Jones had a fair complexion and could often pass as being white, a trait that he would use to his advantage.

In 1837, at the age of twenty, Jones moved to Tuscaloosa, where he married Evalina Love, who was also a free person of color. This would be important for the couple's children because as the rules of the day dictated, the status of the mother determined the status of the children. In this case, Evalina was a free black woman, so her children—eventually fourteen of them—were also free.

At this time, Tuscaloosa was the capital of the newest state in the Union, Alabama. The population grew considerably, as did the need for new buildings and infrastructure. Hundreds of freemen, mostly artisans skilled in plaster work, came to the city for work. But other services were needed as well, including barbers to tend to the grooming of elected officials and businessmen who would be coming to the city. Many of the barbershops across the state were owned and operated by free blacks. It is estimated that during this time period, half of the barbershops in Mobile were owned and operated by these men who offered to their white customers an ear, casual small talk, a good haircut and, most importantly, flattery. One of the most successful barbers in Tuscaloosa was named James Abbott.

Although the records aren't exactly clear on this, it appears that Jones was an apprentice in Abbott's shop in 1837 and later took over ownership. One thing Jones was good at was listening, and he would often glean bits and pieces of information about bargain real estate deals that were coming on the market. With that information, Jones began building his wealth.

According to the 1850 census, Jones had $500 worth of real estate, but that increased to $7,000 by the end of the decade.

In addition to being a barber, Jones was an ordained minister with the AME Zion Church and a believer that free blacks would fare better outside of the United States in Africa in the tiny country of Liberia.

In 1821, a group of white Americans, including some slaveholders, formed a group called the American Colonization Society (ACS). The members, including some prominent Americans like Henry Clay and Francis Scott Key, believed that slavery was not sustainable and would eventually be abolished. But they also believed that free slaves shouldn't remain here and should instead be sent back to their homeland. ACS purchased a tract of land on the east coast of Africa from local tribes with the goal of relocating freed slaves and later free blacks to the new country, Liberia.

In 1830, the Alabama chapter of ACS was formed. In an 1837 edition of the society's newspaper, the *Independent Repository*, slaveholder James Gillespie Bernie penned an article saying that "colonization was a noble benevolence that would lift all bars to fellow man's enjoyment of life and liberty in the land of their fathers."

After reading words like those in the *Repository*, Jones became enamored of the idea of a country where free blacks could set up their own laws, build their own cities and live completely free. Jones would champion the idea of the colonization of Liberia for several decades.

Personally, though, for one reason or another, the dream of relocating to Liberia was always just out of reach for Jones, mainly due to the fact that he had to keep his business and real estate interests going. Many free blacks in Alabama agreed that Liberia would be the land where they could truly be free, but they sat back and waited to see what their like-minded friends would do—would they immigrate or not? If they did, what did they find in the new land?

The dream of colonizing Liberia not only appealed to Jones and free blacks but also to two other very different groups, each for its own reasons. Those who opposed slavery—abolitionists—became disillusioned with their cause and began to feel that abolition would never become a reality. They believed that maybe free blacks moving to Liberia would be the best for them.

Colonization also appealed to slaveholders who saw free blacks as rebels. They set bad examples for slaves and could eventually cause an insurrection against their owners. For all three groups, it was a win-win situation.

By 1848, as the state capital was moved from Tuscaloosa to Montgomery, Jones had become the leading proponent of colonization in the state, speaking with many free blacks in north Alabama and Tennessee about the benefits and prospects of such a move. In September 1850, Jones wrote to Washington and asked that the federal government commission the building of several large steamer ships to facilitate this migration. In the letter, he wrote, "I candidly believe that within 10 years of the first trip that there will not be a free man of color left in the Southern or slaveholding states."

Up to this time, colonization was all talk, and nothing much came of it. By 1851, many whites had begun to think the organization was strictly an abolitionist group determined to end slavery. Because of this sentiment, ACS reworded its mission statement so there would be no doubt—it would "promote the immigration of free colored people from the state of Alabama to Africa and *not* slaves."

Still, the feeling that the society was going to undermine the institution of slavery was growing across the state. Letters that appeared in newspapers in Mobile, Montgomery and Tuscaloosa bolstered those sentiments: "Free blacks in the same community with slaves is a source of evil," one said. "Black churches are the rallying points where the black villains caucus and create their plans for rascality for the coming week," another said. Still others proclaimed that "barbershops provided incendiary circulars and abolitionist rhetoric." Even black churches were cited as the root of evil in the land of slavery: "The sooner the negro churches of our city [Tuscaloosa] are closed the better."

To many whites, Shandy Jones was the most dangerous of free blacks—a financially successful barber who was also a minister. They believed that he and others like him would upend slavery by making clandestine plans in the barbershops and preaching their antislavery rhetoric in the churches. This couldn't be further from the truth, but once a seed is planted…

The call went out for the removal of all free blacks from the state or to have them sold into servitude. Nothing came of it, but in Tuscaloosa, an ordinance was passed stating that free blacks had to register with the mayor and post a one-hundred-dollar "security." Additionally, a curfew of 10:00 p.m. was imposed on them unless they had a special pass from the mayor.

Nothing is known about Jones's life during the Civil War, although we do know that his son was a soldier in the Confederate army. When the war ended and the Confederacy fell, many slaves simply walked off their plantations and headed to cities to find work, while others went into "negotiations" with their former owners to continue working but with concessions such as decent food, clothing, shelter and healthcare. There were calls for integrated schools with the belief that if the races learned together then the hatred would end.

In May 1866, Jones came to Mobile to attend a conference of the AME Zion Church. Here, he was fully ordained and sent back to Tuscaloosa to establish three black churches. This was the period of Reconstruction, a dark, dismal and bitter time in the eyes of many Southerners. In the following year, the Republican-led Congress in Washington put Alabama under military rule until the state could craft a new constitution, approve a referendum to allow blacks to vote and ratify the Fourteenth Amendment to the Constitution granting citizenship to former slaves. In a short time, these measures were approved, and one year later, Shandy Jones did the unthinkable—he ran in Alabama's Fourth District for a seat in the U.S. Congress.

No one knows why, but Jones dropped out of the race only to run and win election soon after as one of the first black members of the Alabama State House of Representatives.

This did not sit well with many whites in the state. For the first time, the state's black newspaper, the *Alabama Nationalist*, warned of a group called the Ku Klux Klan and told its readers that if attacked, it was their right to defend themselves from these radicals. The editor of the *Tuscaloosa Independent Monitor*, Ryland Randolph, ramped up the rhetoric, especially against Jones. Randolph praised a competing black barbershop in Tuscaloosa in his newspaper, calling it the "white folks barber" and that it would be the only one left if the "K-K-Ghosts" remain about. He also blasted whites who patronized "the insolent gorilla Shandy Jones instead of the K-K-Barber."

In 1868, with business at his shop in sharp decline, Jones once again touted the idea of colonization, stating, "There is not a shadow of hope for equal rights and justice in this land."

Even though disillusioned, Jones continued his work in the statehouse. Making a speech on the steps of Tuscaloosa's courthouse, Jones asked why white people would object to having their children at school with colored children as long as the parents of black children didn't object.

Randolph exploded again, writing in his paper, "He [Jones] should have been Ku-Kluxed right there!"

On September 1, Randolph published a now infamous cartoon. Titled, *A Prospective Scene in the City of Oaks, 4th of March, 1869*, the cartoon was a threat to those who were considered enemies and what would happen to them if the Democratic candidate for president of the United States, Horatio Seymour, was not elected. You need to remember that during this time, Republicans

A cartoon threatening that the KKK would lynch scalawags, carpetbaggers and freemen if Horatio Seymour became president of the United States. *Public domain.*

were more aligned with the idea of abolitionism and freedom for all, while Democrats were the polar opposite.

Pictured in the cartoon is a Democratic donkey with the letters **KKK** printed on its side. From the long arm of a tree, two men hang. The first is a "carpetbagger" (a Northerner who came to the South to profit on Reconstruction), the Reverend Arad S. Larkin, who had just been named the president of the newly established University of Alabama. The other was a "scalawag" (a Republican who collaborated with the North), Dr. Noah B. Cloud, who had just been named the superintendent of public instruction in Alabama.

Shandy Jones doesn't appear in the cartoon, but the caption that appeared beneath it puts him squarely in the scene: "PS—It will be seen that there is room left on the limb for the suspension of any bad grant Negro who may be found at the propicoious [*sic*] moment." Randolph labeled Jones the greatest rascal among all of the black men of Tuscaloosa.

But Randolph wasn't finished yet. He printed another cartoon, depicting Jones's son, the former Confederate soldier, as a gorilla climbing Jones's barber pole. As the 1870 elections rolled around, Randolph wrote that Jones should be beaten with a hickory stick and banished from Tuscaloosa. Jones was handily defeated in his reelection bid.

Fearing for his life, Jones retreated into hiding in the southern part of Tuscaloosa and moved on to Mobile with his wife and children. Sadly, his wife of thirty-three years, Evalina, died shortly after the move. Jones did remarry and obtained what was considered the most important job in Mobile, collector for the Port of Mobile, a very prestigious and profitable position.

In 1883, Jones was listed as the minister of the Little Zion Church located on the corner of Church and Bayou Streets. Three years later, on January 31, while relaxing at home, Jones told church elders he was dying. Two days later, he quietly passed away.

Not long ago, after hearing the story of Shandy Jones, the nonprofit Friends of Magnolia set out to find his grave, and in 2015, it was located—the final resting place of one of the state's most influential freemen of color, a man who worked tirelessly for freedom not for some but for all people of color in the state, the Reverend Shandy Jones.

16

THE ICE MAN COMETH. LITERALLY.

Y ou have already read about the struggles of the early colonists at Fort Louis de la Louisiane (Mobile) fighting the heat, disease and food shortages. Famine was of chief concern to those early Mobilians, and many times the meals they ate were simple vegetable dishes or Indian corn (maize), but when they were able to hunt for meat, storing it was a challenge. There was basically only one method—curing—which could be done in a number of ways, such as drying, brining or salting. It could be quite a cumbersome and laborious process, and if not done right, rations wouldn't last long in the subtropical Mobile climate.

Apparently knowing when to cure meat and how long it would keep was complicated as well, so much so that Elizabeth Hammond wrote an extremely popular book on the subject in 1819 called *Modern Domestic Cookery and Useful Receipt Book Adapted for Families in the Middling and Genteel Ranks of Life.* Quite a title, but the information within attempted to simplify things:

> *Beef is never out of season all the year round, though for salting and hanging it is best from Michaelmas (the Feast of Michael observed in September) to Lady Day (the Feast of Annunciation celebrated in March). Mutton is in season from Mid-August till by May; grass lamb, May till September; house lamb is in high season at Christmas but very good from October to May. Pork comes in season at Michaelmas and continues so till April; but hams and bacon are never out of season when carefully cured. Veal from its speedy decay in hot or close weather is generally allowed to be best from Christmas to June.*

In the late 1800s and early 1900s, ice became a more convenient method to keep meat, fruits and vegetables fresh, but without today's conveniences such as refrigerators and icemakers in Mobile, where would you get the commodity? Why, Maine, of course.

Benjamin D. Baker was employed as a writer during the Great Depression with the government's Works Progress Administration (WPA) Federal Writer's Project. People tend to forget that during the Depression, the government created not only thousands of jobs for unemployed workers through programs like the Civilian Conservation Corps (CCC) but also programs that hired artists and writers to document American history.

In late 1939, Baker came to Mobile and recorded interviews and stories with many Mobilians about life in the Port City, both past and during the Depression. One of his more interesting interviews was with Captain John Dorgan, a tugboat captain who sailed the bay and rivers of Mobile. During his conversation with Dorgan, Baker discovered that Mobile received all of its ice by imports from Maine.

In the dead of winter, huge blocks of ice would be cut away from deep packs in one of the northernmost areas of the continental United States. The ice was stored in insulated warehouses until spring and summer, when it was loaded onto ships on the Kennebec River, sailed to the Atlantic Ocean and down to Mobile.

Mobile had only one storage facility that could keep the ice from melting, and that was the fruit wharf (what was commonly referred to as the Banana Docks), where giant shipments of fruits like bananas would be unloaded and stored before being loaded onto refrigerated railcars for distribution across the country.

Dorgan remembered that there was no delivery service at the time unless you owned a butcher shop or saloon. "It was a common sight, in the summer months, to see Negro boys parading down Dauphin Street with ice held by string."

Shipping ice was a dangerous job. "I remember when it took as long as 54 days for the schooners and brigs to make the voyage to Mobile. Sometimes the ice would melt more in one end of the ship than in the other and the vessel would come into port off balance. I have seen as many as seven ships loaded with ice here in one day. They were small vessels and did not carry more than two or three hundred tons."

Dorgan said that the amount of ice the city could obtain was limited because of the bay—it was very shallow. It could take a ship four to five days to sail up the bay to the city.

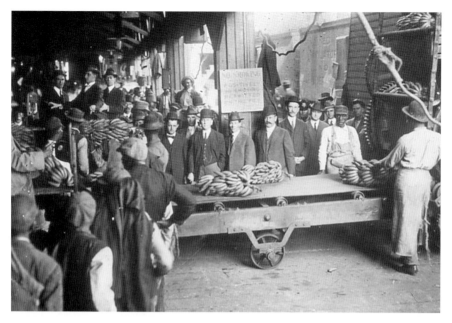

The only place where Mobile's supply of ice could be stored in the early 1900s, the Fruit (Banana) Docks. *Mobile Public Library Local History & Genealogy.*

"Ships drawing more than twelve feet could not come in here then," he said. "That is the reason we did not get more ice at a time. They had to go around and up the Spanish River and then back down the Mobile River to get to the city."

It wasn't until 1885 that a ship with a seventeen-foot draft could safely sail up the bay. By the 1920s, the ship channel was deepened to thirty feet.

Mobile wasn't the only Gulf Coast city that relied on these ice shipments. New Orleans did, too, and once, it suffered an "ice famine."

"They were in a bad way down there and needed ice," Dorgan said. "They telegraphed Mobile and had all the tugs and towboats in the Gulf lookout for an ice vessel they were expecting. They offered a big reward to the one bringing the vessel into New Orleans."

17

FABULOUS FRASCATI PARK

Two miles south of the intersection of Water and Dauphin Streets in downtown Mobile, there is a small peninsula of land that juts out into Mobile Bay that is part of McDuffie Island. The area is known as Choctaw Point.

This area has been popular with Mobilians since the city's dawning. In 1711, one of the town founders, Jean-Baptiste Le Moyne de Bienville, built what many during that period would have thought to have been a mansion considering the wild and primitive environment where it was built. The Chateau Bienville was constructed just south of Choctaw Point at Garrow's Bend. This hand-hewn log home was considered Bienville's summer house and had a beautiful view of Mobile Bay to the east. The home was furnished with an armoire, tables, chairs and a bed. The property itself was lined with magnificent flowering and fragrant magnolia trees, Spanish moss–draped live oaks and a variety of fruit and nut trees, including persimmons, walnuts and cherry. From his porch, he could track shipping coming in and out of the harbor.

It was here at this same location, over one hundred years later, that one of the largest and most popular public parks in the city was built—Frascati Park.

The park was made possible when Conception Street was completed. In 1849, the street was extended from downtown south an additional two miles, where it connected with a road that skirted the beautiful waters of Mobile Bay. This road was made up of hard-packed broken oyster shells and, for obvious reasons, became known as Bay Shell Road. Along Bay Shell Road, there was a sprinkling of houses, nurseries, several refreshment establishments and a horse racing track, the Magnolia Race Course.

This postcard depicts a horse-drawn carriage meandering down Bay Shell Road on its way to Frascati Park. *Detroit Photographic Company.*

The first recorded mention of building a park here at Choctaw Point is found in newspaper accounts from 1855 when it was reported that several proposals were being put forth. An unnamed but "well-known businessman" told the press, "One of the most beautiful public parks in the country could be made at Frascati, fronting the water, making a perfect panorama of picturesque Mobile Bay."

Indeed, the chosen site was a picture postcard of what people envisioned life in Mobile to be like, the same vision that Bienville had pictured one hundred years' prior—cool bay breezes continually blowing in from the east, the gnarled limbs of live oaks gracefully adorned with flowing Spanish moss and the fragrant perfume of those flowering magnolias filling the air.

The proprietor of Mobile's elegant Battle House Hotel, Henry Nabring, acquired several parcels of land on the point. Fifteen of those acres were set aside for developing the park, which he called Frascati after the Italian village that is famous for its Villa Torlonia fountain and Villa Aldobrandini garden.

Nabring fell on tough financial times in late 1869, and the land was turned over to Martin Horst in 1870. This European immigrant would see that the park was completed and that it was developed into a major hub of entertainment with baseball fields, an open air pavilion, concessions and a long pier that extended out into the bay. Horst also brought in remarkable landscaping and an ornate fountain, attempting to bring its gardens up to the quality of its legendary namesake in Italy.

Eventually, a horse-drawn streetcar made regular trips from downtown to the park, making the turnaround for the return trip at the park's fountain. A reporter for the *Daily Register* described a trip to the park in May 1891:

> *A trip to South End, either by boat or the Bay Shell Road, will be found one of the pleasantest journeys out of the city during the summer. The resort itself is one of the pleasantest and best conducted places you can visit. The water salty, the bathing delightful, with good fishing off the boathouse wharf. The grounds are cool and amply shaded, with delightful nooks and summer houses for small or large parties.*

One year after taking charge of the property, Horst was voted in as the city's mayor.

Frascati was the center of family-friendly entertainment in Mobile. That family-friendly atmosphere was only strengthened when in 1888 the state's General Assembly in Montgomery passed into law an act that strictly prohibited "drunken, disorderly, mischievous, lewd, or other improper person or persons [on park grounds]." Punishment would be no more than one hundred dollars and accommodations in the county jail for no more than six months.

In modern-day Mobile, Mobilians know that there are two types of racetracks in town: stock car racing at the Mobile International Speedway and greyhound racing at Mobile Greyhound Park. Over a century ago, before these two tracks were built, Mobile had two first-class horse racing tracks, one of those based at Frascati Park.

William Cotrill, a British immigrant to the United States, came to Mobile in 1841 and opened a successful butcher shop with his brother-in-law. Cotrill was fascinated with all things equestrian and took part in a number of events at the city's Bascombe Race Course, where it is believed he rode in the country's first hurdle race.

During the Civil War, Cotrill used his equestrian skills as a captain with a Confederate cavalry unit. Following the war, he turned his attention to raising Thoroughbred racehorses—hundreds of them, in fact—and purchased the Magnolia Race Course at Frascati.

The track and breeding business proved quite successful for Cotrill, and with his earnings, he went on to build a new track in Long Branch, New Jersey, where his horses tallied wins up and down the Eastern Seaboard. His greatest win was with his horse Buchanan, which won the 1884 Kentucky Derby.

Just as a side note, Saratoga Race Track in New York wanted to name one of its races after the successful businessman. The modest Cotrill declined the honor, so the track named a race in honor of his home state, the Alabama Stakes, which is still run to this very day.

Frascati also had a baseball diamond that fielded some of Mobile's earliest baseball teams, such as the Acid Iron Earth team and the Swamp Angels. And decades before the Negro League was formed, Frascati's ballpark hosted several early black teams from Mobile, including the Mobile Spiders.

The Spiders played teams along the central Gulf Coast from New Orleans to Pensacola with only a single line or two of newsprint devoted to their games in the local papers. The *New Orleans Times-Picayune* gave the team a little more type in its October 1, 1894 edition:

> *The two crack colored clubs of this city, the Alabamas and Mobiles [Spiders], played the second game of a championship series of five games at Frascati this afternoon, in the presence of an audience composed of 100 white and 900 Negroes. The game was exciting from start to finish, and was won by the Alabamas, who have won both games. The batteries were White and Sanders for the Alabamas, and Nicholas and Smith for the Mobiles. Randolph umpired a good game. The score was 15 to 9.*

Not only was Frascati a great place for swimming, picnicking, and taking in a baseball game, it was a cultural hub for the city as well. When the nation celebrated its centennial in 1876, the park hosted its own celebration with German marching bands, local singers, dancing and speeches.

A favorite of Mobilians was the Frascati Theater's offering of light operatic performances. One touring group that frequented the theater was the J.H. Huntley Comedy Company. The company toured across the country, performing several different plays in a single city for a few days or an entire season. In the spring of 1892, for example, the company performed the plays *Dens and Palaces*, *Rip Van Winkle*, *The Galley Slave*, *The Convict*, *Uncle Daniel* and, years later, Jules Verne's *Michael Strogoff*. No, *Strogoff* is not a science fiction tale. It is the story of a captain in the czar of Russia's army during the Tatar Revolution.

Probably the most famous name to grace the Frascati stage was Irish poet and playwright Oscar Fingal O'Flahertie Wills Wilde, better known to the world simply as Oscar Wilde.

Best known for his novel *The Picture of Dorian Gray*, Wilde was a flamboyant dresser with a clever, quick wit that charmed the country during his tour of the United States in 1882. He brought to the country his view that art exists for the sake of its beauty alone—aestheticism.

It seemed odd that such a personality would come to Mobile, but he did, and the city was enthusiastic to receive the poet, to say the least. When tickets went on sale at Soto and Primo's drugstore at the corner of Dauphin and Royal Streets, all three hundred tickets sold out in a flash. The going price for reserve seat tickets was seventy-five cents.

The local press, however, was skeptical about Wilde's appearance, but by the time he exited the stage, the *Mobile Register* had joined the city in praising Wilde's appearance: "We confess to have gone to Frascati with decided prejudice against Mr. Wilde, but candor compels us to admit that such prejudice was unfounded."

While in Mobile, Wilde wanted to pay a call on famous author Augusta Evans Wilson. While Wilson was a gracious host to most visitors and admirers, she did grow weary of them constantly coming to her door to meet her. She once told a friend that she felt like a "two headed calf in a circus side show." Wilson refused to entertain Wilde, saying that his lifestyle defamed his art.

Frascati Park was operated by Horst until his death in 1878. His widow retained the property and continued to run the park with the aid of a man identified only as "Mr. Kennedy." Kennedy contracted many acts to perform at the park, lined up its baseball schedule, installed swings for children and adults and added refreshment stands, anything to ensure that the crowds kept coming.

Mrs. Horst decided to sell the property in 1891. Several African American businessmen made overtures to buy the park and turn it into a resort for, as the newspapers said, "a place for people of their race," but nothing came of the effort. Eventually, the family sold the property to D.R. Burgess on May 24, 1891.

Sadly, Frascati's heyday came to an end with the hurricane of 1906 that pummeled the city and the Gulf Coast, destroying the park's entire infrastructure and the city's first entertainment complex. The park never recovered, and soon after, the Gulf, Mobile and Northern Railroad took possession of the land and erected shops where it could maintain their railway cars. Today, there are no vestiges of the old park.

Years later, a local bank presented a short piece on Frascati Park, and although it was an advertisement for a bank that was placed in a long since forgotten magazine, the final paragraph of the ad summarized the spirit of this park nicely:

> *When we think of Frascati…we are reminded of the many gay times had there, of the pleasures of recreation, of the importance of enjoying a carefree vacation.*

18

SCENES OF DESTRUCTION

Alabama has a gorgeous but small shoreline along the Gulf of Mexico with brilliant turquoise waters that are outlined by pristine white sand beaches. Tall sea oats sway lazily in the breeze atop dunes. Mobile is located only a few short miles north of that shoreline. That footprint of land along the Gulf Coast is relatively small as compared to the other Gulf states, except for Mississippi, that is, which has about the same size shoreline. While Alabama's gulf-side footprint is small, it has still seen some major and devastating hurricanes crash on those snowy white beaches over the centuries.

If you live along the Gulf Coast, the joke is that you don't remember years when something happened, you remember the hurricanes. Ask anyone from Mobile where they were in late summer of 1979, and odds are they will say, "Oh, you mean the Frederic year."

And everyone has a story to tell about the storms that they experienced—Frederic, Ivan, Katrina, Camille. These are only a few of the many that immediately come to mind. Some of those storms were direct hits, coming in straight from the Gulf to cause considerable damage and deaths, while others came in on an angle, usually arriving from the southwest heading northeast, sometimes leaving more death and destruction in their wake than a direct hit.

While the hurricanes I just mentioned are still fresh in Mobile's collective memory, there are many others that have ravaged Mobile that are now only distant memories, if remembered at all. For one thing, storms were not given official names by the World Meteorological Society until 1953, although some Caribbean islands would name their own storms after saints, like Hurricane Santa Ana, which struck Puerto Rico in 1876. Otherwise, until the formalization of a naming system, all hurricanes were known as "no-name" storms or by the year they struck.

Two of those no-name storms hit the Port City and the Gulf Coast in the late 1800s and early 1900s. One of the two made landfall near the Mississippi-Alabama state line in 1906.

For those of you who have never experienced a hurricane, the most destructive winds are not necessarily where the eye makes landfall but rather on the northeast side of the storm, and that was what was gunning for the Port City on September 26, 1906.

The storm began as a tropical depression on September 19 in the western Caribbean off the Yucatán Peninsula. The depression slowly meandered north–northwest across the gulf, gaining strength along the way until mariners reported the storm just off the U.S. coast on September 24 with maximum winds of 75 miles an hour—what we now call a category 1 storm. But it wasn't finished developing. By early that evening, its maximum winds had reached 120 miles an hour, a category 3 storm.

Mobile was more fortunate than most Gulf Coast cities. The city was one of the first to play host to what would become the National Weather Service (NWS). The service began when a joint resolution by Congress was signed by Ulysses S. Grant on February 9, 1870, authorizing the secretary of war to provide "the taking of meteorological observations at military stations in the interior of the continent and at other points in the states and territories." Later in the year, the first observations were telegraphed by sergeants of the Army Signal Service at twenty-two locations across the country. Mobile was one of those first twenty-two cities to be selected as a site.

Still, the science of predicting the weather and hurricanes was primitive, to say the least. While scientific principles were employed for basic forecasts, it was still a guessing game when it came to the severity of approaching storms and where they would make landfall. There were no satellites or radar, so those living on the coast had little to no warning of the danger they were in.

On the morning of September 26, simple red flags flew over the local weather bureau office at the customshouse on the corner of Royal and St. Francis Streets to indicate that the NWS had noticed a change in the barometric pressure and a storm was approaching. The following morning, Mobilians were greeted with the full force of the storm.

Although winds had died down to 110 miles an hour, it still carried a big punch. The system's barometric pressure upon landfall was recorded at 977 millibars in Mobile.

Roofs, signs, shingles, trees, chimneys—they were no match for the wind. The main street that follows the shoreline of Mobile Bay along the Port City's docks, which is appropriately named Water Street, became just that—the water from the bay was being pushed north into the Mobile River, which overflowed its banks and turned the street into its own river. News reports called the street a "surging maelstrom."

Walter Bellingrath, who at the time had one of the most successful Coca-Cola bottling franchises in the country, had located a warehouse and his first bottling facility on Water Street. The plant had its roof severely damaged, and merchandise was washed away. In a letter to his brother, he wrote that "the next time they hang out that weather flag, I'm going to leave town!"

Along with eleven steamships and schooners sunk in Mobile Bay, the steamer ship *Camp Carney* was tossed over Water Street, landing at the foot of St. Francis Street. Telegraph wires were cut, knocking out communications. When the storm had passed, it was estimated that damages totaled over $15 million and 150 people had died in Mississippi, Florida and Alabama.

Most hurricanes that make their way to Mobile are not direct hits, where the eye of the storm passes directly over the city. These storms tend to ram the coast at an angle, coming in from either the east or west, then make a slight turn to skirt the coastline once it makes initial landfall. When this happens along the central Gulf Coast, you can bet that Mobile will see at least some of its effects.

That was the case in 1893 when a strong unnamed storm plowed northward over the warm gulf waters, heading for a date with the coast. Once again, as is the case with most late-season hurricanes, a disturbance formed off the Yucatan Peninsula on the morning of September 27. Two days later, it passed the peninsula and surged into the warm gulf, where it quickly gained strength, with winds topping 133 miles an hour. The storm was initially heading toward landfall along the Louisiana-Texas border, but a cold front changed its direction, and by October 1, it was turning, taking a northeasterly track toward the Louisiana-Mississippi border.

The first feeder bands and gusty winds brushed the Louisiana coast as the day dawned, pelting the coast with wave after wave of rain until the next morning, when all hell broke loose.

Just west of Grand Isle, Louisiana, there was a small town called Cheniere Caminada. According to church records, in 1893, the tiny coastal village had

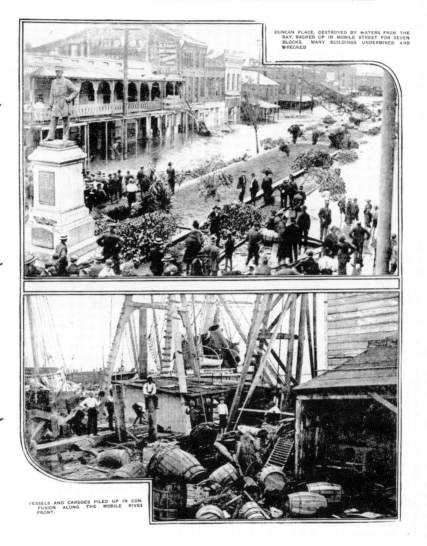

The damage the 1906 hurricane wreaked on Mobile was immense. Decades later, the National Weather Service declared it a strong category 2 storm. *Library of Congress Prints and Photographs Division.*

a population of 1,471. As the storm pushed onward, it created an eighteen-foot storm surge, sweeping away all but one house in the small town and killing 779 people—over half of the town's population.

But the storm wasn't finished yet. It began to curve toward the east, battering the Mississippi coast before heading to Mobile. While the wind caused much damage to the city, most of the destruction was due to severe flooding, as once again, the storm pushed the waters of Mobile Bay and all five rivers that feed the bay and the delta upstream. The waters rose with incredible speed, causing panic among residents. It was reported that streams were filled with furniture floating by and railroad lines were cut off, their tracks having been washed away by the flood waters. Bay Shell Road along the bay's western shoreline was completely destroyed, washed away from over six inches of rain. Telegraph communications were disrupted—as reporters noted, "There was barely a pole left standing."

In downtown Mobile, along the waterfront, the Mobile River rose fast enough that people could easily watch its advance. Business owners rushed to move inventory to upper floors. By 10:00 a.m., the water had covered Water Street and continued flowing another quarter of a mile inland to Royal Street.

Several steamer ships were washed ashore, including the *Crescent City*, *Lee* and *Lotus*. One ship, however, wasn't able to survive the storm. The schooner, *Alice Graham*, capsized and sank only two miles off of Cedar Point. All hands on board were lost.

While the storm devastated the city proper, across Mobile Bay on its eastern shore, residents were reporting "nothing but devastation and destruction." Houses were either blown away, like those at Cedar Point, where twenty-five were laid to waste by the wind or by the rising water. The water rose so fast that a headline in the *Daily Register* asked the question, "Was It a Tidal Wave?"

The reports from the Mobile-Tensaw River delta brought horrific news:

> *On the marsh, the loss of life is appalling. Whole families have been swept out of existence and the actual number of the lost will never be known.*

One Eastern Shore resident, Earnest Miller, recalled his harrowing experience to the *Daily Register*. Miller and his wife, who was "crazed with fright," had managed to evacuate their home, which was submerged in water. They were able to make their way to their son-in-law's house, where three men, five women, two children and an eight-month-old baby were waiting out the storm—at least that was the plan until the waters of the Mobile-Tensaw River delta began to fill their house:

> *We all remained in the house until 2 o'clock when the wind kept increasing and blew out and carried away the doors and windows. I was standing in water up to my armpits and the waves were continuously washing over my head. The women and children were almost strangled by the salt water. We then began the perilous task of transferring the women and children to boats [that were tied to the house]. We finally got everybody out of the house. We remained in this situation, exposed to the fury of the wind and waves and the drenching rain for two long hours.*

A reporter for the *Register* took a boat across the bay, where he rescued several German children who were tied together to a tree, apparently lashed there by their parents to keep them from floating away from one another in the flood waters. Their parents were never found.

As the storm downgraded to a tropical storm and then a subtropical system over Georgia, residents began assessing the damages. In downtown Mobile, owners of storefronts that were inundated with mud and silt from the bay were quick to roll up their sleeves and get to work with the cleanup as soon as the water began to recede. One reporter marveled at the work being done and resilience of Mobilians:

> *The inundated portion of the city early presented an animated appearance and the work of cleaning out the muddy sediment deposited in stores by the receding water was pushed with that energy and vigor that characterizes the average Mobilian.*

Total damages for the 1893 storm, now known as the Cheniere Caminada Hurricane in honor of the people and town virtually lost in Louisiana, were estimated to have been over $5 million. The storm was responsible for over two thousand deaths, making this previously unnamed storm the fourth deadliest in U.S. history.

19

THE BEAT OF THE BAY

There is a musical rhythm to the waters that surround Mobile. From the lightly rippling waters of the Mobile-Tensaw delta that rhythmically slap the knees of cedar trees along the banks of its dark bayous to the crashing, frothing surf of the Gulf of Mexico, there is music in the water.

At one time, that music included the sound of men manually hauling heavy bales of cotton off of steamers in a syncopated cadence along the city's docks. Today, the song of the dock worker has been replaced with the pulsating sound of huge cranes moving giant shipping containers off ships onto flatbeds and railcars.

Whatever the source, there has always been that background of music in the waters surrounding Mobile, and those rhythms have been etched into the souls of some great singers and musicians who came from the Port City—big band trumpeter Charles "Cootie" Williams, jazz trombonist Urbie Green and, of course, Jimmy Buffett.

One musical great who hailed from Mobile has an amazing story to be told. He has been credited as being one of the most respected black bandleaders of all time, creating a unique fusion of ragtime and jazz in the early 1900s. His music, however, often overshadows his incredible military career during World War I. His name is James Reese Europe.

It is interesting to note that Europe's father, Henry, was born into slavery in Mobile in 1847. In 1856, a report was issued by the Mobile Joint Police Commission stating that "it is the opinion of those best informed that there are now in this city as many as 1,000 Negroes who are living apart from their owners or agents." It is believed that Henry was one of those—a slave but living free.

As with most African Americans prior to the Civil War, the Europe family gravitated toward Baptist and Methodist churches, and both Henry and his wife, Lorraine, were very active in the church. At the time, white churches would minister to both free blacks and slaves until they broke off and formed their own congregations. Henry eventually became the pastor of the Virginia Street Church in 1874.

Not much is known about Henry and Lorraine's life during the Civil War, but in the period of Reconstruction, Henry's name appears in records indicating that he had held several jobs, including teacher and writer for the African American newspaper in the city, the *Nationalist*, and spent some time working in the federal government with the Internal Revenue Service and U.S. Post Office, positions he received in part because Republican officials in the federal government "held him in high-esteem."

James Reese Europe was born on born on February 22, 1881. Education for African American children was limited not only in Mobile but also across the South, so, like many others, his mother began teaching her children herself, especially the fundamentals of reading and writing. Later on, they were sent to church-sponsored schools.

Both of James's parents loved music and possessed some musical ability. Writer Charles Welton said that his father, Henry, "could play about everything that would emit a sound when properly coaxed. If a man is going to become the general superintendent of a jazz band, it is always well to select that kind of father."

Both parents played roles in imparting that love to their children. Thanks to their mother, James's sister Mary and brother John became accomplished pianists, and by the time he was nine, James himself was adept at playing the piano as well as improvising on the fiddle and banjo. James also fell in love with the sounds of Mobile's brass cadet marching bands. These drill teams appeared in Mobile in the late 1800s and would tour the country, often taking first place in competitions. The sounds of the blaring horns could be heard up and down the shoreline of Mobile Bay in the evenings.

When James turned nine years old, the Europe family packed up and moved north to Washington, D.C., but the seeds of future musical accomplishments and worldwide success had been planted along the banks of Mobile Bay.

In 1904, James turned his sights toward the bright lights of the entertainment mecca of the world, New York City. He moved to the Big Apple when he turned twenty-three years old. As a pianist, he found it easy to pick up work with black theater groups and felt quite at home there. As he settled into this new world, James began composing his own music, and two years after arriving in the city, one of his first songs, "Gay Luneta," was picked up and used by famed African American Broadway producers Cole and Johnson in their play *Shoe-Fly Regiment*. Almost overnight, Europe was making quite a name for himself in the city, with several more of his songs appearing in other Broadway productions. In 1908, he became the musical director for Cole and Johnson's production of, *The Red Moon*.

It was at this point that James decided to channel his newfound fame toward helping other African American musicians further their careers and garner work. In 1910, he formed a combination band and musicians' union—the Clef Club. The club acted as an agency, helping black artists land gigs around the region. The band, known as the Clef Club Symphony Orchestra, consisted of 125 members, including 47 mandolins, 27 harp guitars and plenty of banjos.

Europe held a deep belief that African American music was important and that only African Americans should play it, not all-white bands. In the same sense, though, he believed that their music should be heard by all races. And with that, on May 2, 1912, the Clef Club orchestra played Carnegie Hall with a performance titled *A Concert of Negro Music*.

Europe went on to form a second similar organization in 1913, the Tempo Club, and began playing swanky upscale dance clubs that had become all the rage throughout the city. It was during this time that he met up with musician and composer Noble Sissle. The two became fast friends, and together, they wrote music and played the piano at some of the richest white parties in the city. But while they had become the toast of high society, they still faced many indignations like having to enter the mansions through the back door.

With all of this fame and success, Europe began rubbing elbows with some of the biggest names in the entertainment world, including Vernon and Irene Castle. The Castles were a husband-and-wife dance team who gained worldwide fame by popularizing such dances as the Glide, the Castle Walk and the Tango. Europe began a partnership with the pair, and the result was the creation of the dances the Turkey Trot and Fox Trot.

Europe's music had morphed into something more than just the popular ragtime of the day. His music had become a unique and complex fusion of ragtime and jazz, something never heard before, and it didn't go unnoticed. In 1914, Europe was invited to the Victor Recording Company's studios to put his music down on vinyl. Although not the first African American to make a recording (that honor went to former slave George W. Johnson, who was discovered singing on the streets of Washington, D.C., in 1890), he was one of the earliest. Europe's song "The One Step Rag" (aka "The Castle House Rag") was added to the National Registry of Recordings in 2004. The recording is described as "exciting" and "vigorously driven by aggressive drumming."

By the time his recording contract with Victor ran out, there was a sharp and noticeable rise in the number of black instrumental groups that were making records. Europe had led the way.

But it wasn't only this early musical success that brought Europe fame. His service on the battlefield and with wounded troops during World War I captured the hearts of the French, British, General John J. Pershing and, eventually, Americans who still had a hard time accepting an integrated military or who harbored racist attitudes.

Europe's military career begins on June 2, 1913, when, after considerable pushback from white representatives, the New York state legislature finally passed a bill that authorized the formation of African American National Guard units. The bill was signed into law by Governor William Sulzer, and almost immediately, the Fifteenth New York Colored Infantry Regiment was established. The unit would be composed of soldiers from Harlem.

The unit did not begin filling out its ranks until two years later. Up until then, Europe resisted enlisting, believing that segregation in the military offered little hope of opportunities for blacks. But, as he said, the military provided an opportunity for those who did join to create a "strong, powerful institution for the development of the Negro manhood of Harlem. Our race will never amount to anything, politically or economically, in New York or anywhere else unless there are strong organizations of men who stand for something in the community."

To say that Europe was a busy man in 1916 is an understatement. At this time, he had sixteen bands under his direction and continued to play wealthy white parties. Even with all of this going on, Europe announced to Sissle that he would be joining the army. Sissle reminded Europe that he had this musical empire to tend to and that he didn't have time for the army. Europe looked at his friend and told him that he would be joining, too.

After a little persuasion, Sissle signed up as well. Europe was commissioned as a lieutenant after passing the officer exam and headed a machine gun company. The unit's commanding officer, Colonel William Hayward—a white man—understood the importance of the Fifteenth and James Reese Europe being in its ranks. He came up with an idea to join Fifteenth New York with another African American National Guard unit, the Eighth Illinois, which already had an incredible band, and assign Europe as the bandleader. Europe knew that his reputation preceded him and told Hayward that he wouldn't do it unless he was given complete freedom to make it the best military band ever.

Hayward agreed, obtained $10,000 in funding to finance the band and appointed Europe the bandleader and Sissle the drum major. The band came together quickly and toured the country and Puerto Rico, recruiting other African Americans along the way.

As the United States entered World War I in 1917, Europe and the Fifteenth were sent to Poughkeepsie, New York, for basic training. The unit began to face more and more racism, beginning with an incident that occurred as the troops were preparing to leave.

Units from twenty-five different states were to march down the city's Fifth Avenue. The parade was called a "rainbow" of states. Colonel Hayward wanted the Fifteenth to be a part of the parade but was told by higher ups that it was a rainbow parade and "black wasn't part of the rainbow."

Once the unit arrived in Poughkeepsie, they faced more racism: a group of white men attacked Sissle as he was buying a newspaper in a hotel lobby. The men of the Fifteenth and an all-white unit came to Sissle's aid and stopped the attackers. Europe stood between Sissle and his assailants until the military police arrived.

Hayward feared for the unit's safety and traveled to Washington to demand that the Fifteenth be relocated to another camp or be deployed immediately to France. Officials in the War Department agreed, and before long, Europe and his unit found themselves in France, where they were assigned to do engineering projects far from the front where the men wanted to be.

Once again, Hayward came to their aid and convinced General John Pershing to move them in to help with the fight. Renamed the 369th Infantry in March 1918, the men of the 15th were attached to the 4th French Army, a unit of the French military that had been fully integrated for years, so the 369th members were quickly accepted as one of their own.

The unit was taught French and the fighting tactics of the French army before being deployed to the Argonne Forest near Champagne in April 1918. The soldiers spent 191 days on the front in combat, longer than any other U.S. unit. The 369th Infantrymen showed their worth, taking on the Germans with ferocity. During one battle, two privates from the unit, Henry Johnson and Neeham Roberts, were attacked by a German patrol. They

Lieutenant James Reese Europe and the 365th Infantry Military Band entertain the patients with real American jazz in the courtyard of a Paris hospital. *Library of Congress American Memory Collection.*

literally fought off two dozen Germans in hand-to-hand combat. Johnson sustained twenty-one wounds. The Germans gave the unit a new name—the Hell Fighters. Europe loved the name, and from then on, the 369th Infantry Band was known as the Hell Fighters.

For over six months, the Hell Fighters fought gallantly. Europe himself was wounded in a gas attack in Maffrécourt, France, and was evacuated back to Paris. While convalescing in the hospital, he wrote the song "On Patrol in No Man's Land." The song was a no-holds-barred word-for-word account of what life was like for the soldiers fighting in France and Germany:

What the time? Nine?
Fall in line
Alright, boys, now take it slow
Are you ready? Steady!
Very good, Eddie.
Over the top, let's go
Quiet, lie it, else you'll start a riot
Keep your proper distance, follow 'long
Cover, brother, and when you see me hover
Obey my orders and you won't go wrong
There's a Minenwerfer coming—
Look out (bang!)
Hear that roar (bang!), there's one more (bang!)
Stand fast, there's a Very light [flare]
Don't gasp or they'll find you all right
Don't start to bombing with those hand grenades (rat-a-tat-tat-tat)
There's a machine gun, holy spades!
Alert, gas! Put on your mask
Adjust it correctly and hurry up fast
Drop! There's a rocket from the Boche barrage
Down, hug the ground, close as you can, don't stand
Creep and crawl, follow me, that's all
What do you hear? Nothing near
Don't fear, all is clear
That's the life of a stroll
When you take a patrol
Out in No Man's Land
Ain't it grand?
Out in No Man's Land

It was here that he also wrote the songs "All of No Man's Land Is Ours" and "How Ya Gonna Keep 'Em Down on the Farm?" The latter is an upbeat little tune that has a subliminal message—how were you going to keep these black soldiers satisfied back home in a land where there was rampant racism and lynching after they had been warmly received and accepted in France?

Eventually, Europe was deemed to be unfit to return to combat, but he still did his part. For the next two months, when the 369th's band was in Paris, the musicians entertained wounded soldiers in camp hospitals and held concerts to tremendous crowds in Paris.

Back on the battlefield, the 369th Infantry suffered devastating losses and casualties in the Second Battle of the Marne before it was reassigned to the French 161st. It was with this new French outfit that the 369th shined, becoming instrumental in the capture of the town of Sechault, France, but the men paid a heavy price for the victory with heavier losses and casualties than in the Second Battle of Marne. The entire band was awarded the Croix de Guerre, the highest award for bravery given by the French government. Additionally, 170 individual medals of valor were presented by France.

The "War to End All Wars" finally came to an end on November 11, 1918. It was another three months before the 369th returned home. The men were surprised to find news of their exploits and heroism on the battlefield spread like wildfire across the United States, and the returning soldiers were greeted as heroes when their ship arrived in New York City.

The unit wasn't allowed to march in the farewell parade years before, but when it was time for the victory parade down the steel and concrete canyons of the city on February 17, 1919, the black soldiers were treated as if they were the guests of honor. Hundreds of thousands lined the streets. Europe proudly led the band with song after song, and when the parade arrived in Harlem, they broke into "Here Comes My Daddy Now."

Almost as soon as Europe and the band had landed back on American soil, they were signed to a recording contract with Pathe Records. He put the music he had written during the war on vinyl, songs that painted a vivid picture of what life was like for soldiers in "no man's land"—the horrors and death they experienced and their prayers that they would get home to see their loved ones once again.

Europe was once again on top of the music world and, with his companion Sissle, set up a national tour of the Hell Fighters' band, including a performance at the New York Opera House.

While preparing for a show in Boston in May 1919, the music came to an end. There are two versions of this story. The first says that following a

Sheet music for "Good Night Angeline," a song written during World War I by James Reese Europe. *Library of Congress American Memory Collection.*

rehearsal, Europe told his drummer, Herbert Wright, to add a little pep to a number. The second story says that Wright felt Europe had cheated him, most likely out of money.

In any case, Wright became upset and stabbed Europe multiple times. Noble Sissle subdued the attacker and waited for police to arrive. To Europe, it looked as if the wounds were not life-threatening, so he told Sissle that he should continue on with the show while he went to the hospital for treatment. Europe died in the hospital early the next morning.

Thousands of people watched as Europe's funeral procession made its way down the New York City streets. The Hell Fighters paraded along with the entourage with instruments in hand, but they did not play. The music had been silenced.

A wreath was to have been placed on his casket by New York governor Calvin Coolidge, but instead, it was placed on the coffin as Europe's body made its way through Harlem.

With Europe's passing, American jazz great Eubie Blake, who actually managed Europe's music business in New York while he was fighting in the war, said of James Reese Europe, "He was our benefactor and inspiration. Even more, he was the Martin Luther King of music."

20

BONE DRY

Prohibition and the Whiskey Trials

B orn to Celebrate." That is the latest marketing slogan for the Port City, and it perfectly sums up the vibe tourists get when they visit Mobile—its rocking downtown nightlife keeps partiers out till the wee hours of the morning and, of course, there is Mardi Gras. In the early 1900s, that celebratory feeling ran into a most formidable foe—the temperance movement and Prohibition.

Eleven years before the entire country went "dry" with the enactment of the Eighteenth Amendment that banned the manufacture, transportation and sale of intoxicating liquors, Alabama decided to give it a go. It did not go over well in the city that was the Mother of Mystics.

In 1907, the Alabama state legislature proposed a new law that would ban the sale of alcohol across the state. The debate that ensued was a heated one, with Mobilians leading the charge against the bill. The passing of such a bill would undermine that celebratory feeling during Mardi Gras and would also affect businesses that catered to sailors coming into port and visitors to the city.

Mobile had a unique religious situation when it came to alcohol and prohibition. While the rest of the state was primarily Methodist and Baptist and would welcome the enactment of the law, in Mobile, which had the largest population of Catholics in the state, the feeling was different, with the Catholic Church turning a blind eye to alcohol. Their belief was that drinking wasn't a sin as long as it was done in moderation.

When the vote to add the law to the state constitution came up, 80 percent of the voters in Mobile voted against the bill, but the rest of the state wasn't on their side and the law went into effect on January 1, 1909. Four months later, while enforcement of the law was fairly lax, there were a few raids sprung on the unsuspecting. In the May 15, 1909 edition of the *Hotel and Employees International Alliance* newsletter, which printed news of interest to its union members, it was reported that:

> *April 8. Wholesale raids by detectives in the employ of the Prohibition party startled the city today, and resulted in the seizure of large quantities of liquors at hotels and cafes. While the officers were searching on place it was discovered that the warrants were defective, and a delay ensued until the error could be rectified. Later the officers visited the new Battle House and the Cawthorn Hotel, where more than a car load of intoxicants were seized. The search was made under the law which forbids the possession of intoxicants for barter. The prohibition law never has been rigidly enforced here.*

Before its repeal, the law did have some financial consequences for the city, like the removal of one of the largest icehouses in Mobile from the Cawthon Hotel, located off Bienville Square at the corner of St. Joseph and St. Francis Streets to Pensacola. It was reported in the January 1910 edition of the trade magazine *Ice and Refrigeration Illustrated*:

> *Owing to the enforcement of prohibition at Mobile, Ala., the Hervey Hotel Co. are moving the 12-ton refrigerating plant, formerly operated at the Cawthon Hotel, Mobile, to the new San Carlos Hotel at Pensacola, the work being under the direction of the Fred W. Wolf Co.*

This first attempt at prohibition didn't last long, however. The law mandated that the sale of alcohol was illegal, not its possession. Realizing the "mistake" they had made in crafting the bill, elected prohibitionist senators and representatives planned to change the law to be all-encompassing—that is, until the Alabama Supreme Court stepped in. The court ruled that alcohol was property and the law cannot prohibit anyone from possessing it as long as it was legally obtained. The law was repealed in 1911, but the battle wasn't over yet.

Following the state elections of 1914, the freshly elected Democratic caucus in both the state House and Senate met on January 12 to discuss the upcoming legislative session and vote on their leadership. Two devout proponents of prohibition were elected: A.H. Carmichael as Speaker of the

House and Thomas L. Bulgar as president of the Senate. Headlines across the state read "Prohibitionists Are in Control of Both Houses." Incoming governor Charles Henderson said he was "surprised" at the strength of the prohibitionist movement in the statehouse.

The following morning, the headlines in the *Mobile Register* rang out, "Liquor Is Doomed in Alabama." During those caucuses in Montgomery, the new political leadership agreed to pass two bills immediately once they were gaveled into session. The first would be a bill that would abolish the Alabama Fish and Game Department. The second would be a law to prohibit the sale and manufacturing of alcohol in the state. The members also pledged to be "honor bound" to back any politician or law that prohibited alcohol.

With incredible swiftness, the temperance committees of both the House and Senate moved the legislation that was crafted by Carmichael to the floor. There was little debate in both chambers, with only a few members allowed to address their colleagues. Mobile's Harry Hartwell led the fight against the bill on the Senate floor to no avail.

In what the press described as a "whirlwind Thursday afternoon," the bill passed the House by a vote of 74–27, the Senate by a vote of 26–9. A second bill that enabled the prohibition law was also adopted by a huge majority. Both bills were sent to outgoing governor Emmet O'Neal's desk. O'Neal simply ignored them, leaving it up to the incoming governor to decide whether to sign them into law. Upon taking office, the new anti-prohibition governor vetoed the bills, sending them back to the House and Senate, where the veto was summarily overridden by the powerful prohibitionist forces. The Carmichael State Prohibition Law, better known as the Bone Dry Law, would go into effect on June 30, 1914.

In true Mobile fashion, alcohol continued to flow in defiance of the law. It was common to see people drinking beer on the front porch of their favorite bar or drugstore. Even Mobile's Mardi Gras societies worked around the law. During Carnival season, it is tradition for a Mystic Society to follow parades with an extravagant party. The masked revelers retire to a ballroom—usually in either the Battle House or the Cawthon Hotels downtown—and host a formal ball where all inhibitions are cast to the wind. If you are not a member of one of these societies, it is an honor to receive an invitation to attend.

During Alabama's bone-dry years, alcohol could not be served in the ballroom itself. So what invited guests would do is show up at the ball and present their invitation at the door, where they would receive a key that opened the door of a room in the hotel where they could partake in libations with their friends.

The swanky Cawthon Hotel featured a rolling bar during Prohibition—roll it into an elevator, then place an out-of-order sign on the door. *Official Hotel Red Book and Directory Company.*

When it came to enforcing the law, particularly those that prohibited the brewing of moonshine or "shiny," the state was fairly lax at first, but rumrunning was another story, as it hit an all-time high. While Alabama has a small footprint on the Gulf Coast, it has hundreds if not thousands of miles of coastline once you consider its myriad rivers, bays, bayous and backwaters. It's the perfect location for smuggling illegal booze into the state. Even today, law enforcement officials will tell you that they grapple with this same situation—today, over one hundred years later, it's illegal drugs and not booze.

In 1918, Mobile's sheriff, William Holcombe, prided himself with busting rumrunners along Alabama's Gulf Coast, telling the *Mobile Register* that it was a "pet activity" of his. On December 23, the sheriff reported hauling in 200, 150 and 145 gallons of mash and whiskey. The following year, the Prohibition Force began ramping up its investigations and reported that the first "shiny" still was captured on Mud Creek off of Moffat Road. The still was described as being "crude," having been made from an iron wash pot, a fire bucket for the top and a wooden base.

This was only the beginning, as the Eighteenth Amendment and the Volstead Act enabling national Prohibition went into effect. In December 1920, the force announced that 337 stills had been captured in Mobile County to date ranging in value from $200 to $300. A spokesman credited the still makers with their skill and ingenuity when it came to building the elaborate stills.

"The girl who can make a boudoir lamp from a parasol has nothing on shiny makers for resourcefulness using gas drums, water boilers, lard cans, and barrels." The deputy went on to say that lye was the main ingredient used to hasten fermentation in these stills, and when the officers arrived on scene, the smell was so strong that it burned their nostrils.

Later that same year, Prohibition agents garnered a warrant and raided the homes of two of the city's wealthiest men. Needless to say, Mobilians went ballistic. Even though he was a prohibitionist, the latest Alabama governor, Thomas Kilby, was feeling the pressure of public opinion resulting from the raid. Kilby was forced to denounce the raid and fired all of those who conducted it. When his prohibition department's chief dissented with the governor's decision, the governor sacked him, too.

Up until this time, things were relatively quiet when it came to enforcing Prohibition laws in Mobile, but on February 28, 1921, the situation turned violent.

It was a peaceful Saturday evening when at 5:00 p.m., sheriff's deputies D.L. Donoghue, Earl Easterling and Walter Blackman were dispatched to a drugstore on Davis Avenue at Lafayette Streets. When they arrived, they were greeted by the owner's son, Malcolm McLaurin. They informed McLaurin that he was in violation of Prohibition laws by selling illegal whiskey, to which McLaurin replied that he would go quietly with them even though he was innocent.

As McLaurin was being placed in the police car, his father, sixty-year-old Dan McLaurin, came out of the store wielding a cane, brandishing a gun and shouting, "Anyone who says my son [broke the law] is a @#%! liar!"

Officer Easterling went over to arrest the elder McLaurin but ended up tussling with him. McLaurin's gun went off, wounding Easterling. The deputy stumbled back, and as he did, McLaurin shot Easterling again, killing the officer. Deputy Blackman rushed McLaurin and grabbed the hand that was holding the gun. It fired again, this time hitting McLaurin. The elder McLaurin was rushed to the hospital, where he later died.

A few years later, a second police officer was killed. The incident occurred once again on Davis Avenue, outside the Pike Theater. Officer Chris Dean was shot and killed by Campbell Starks after the officer engaged a group of people drinking outside the theater. Starks was hanged for the crime five months later, the last legal hanging in the city.

The biggest raid in dry Mobile came when U.S. District Attorney and Mobile County native Aubrey Boyles began his crusade to enforce national Prohibition laws. Boyles was deliberate and determined with his investigations and indictments. It was said that he took particular delight in busting members of the wealthy and powerful Lyons family, who owned a brewery.

One of his first arrests was of a poor elderly woman who was down and out and made what money she could by making and selling beer from her home. "Why are you prosecuting us poor devils," she asked, "when the big fellows are running wild?"

That comment tipped Boyles off that there were bigger fish in the sea, and soon, agents began raiding businesses where they found that store owners were paying local wholesalers for imported liquor. The wholesalers, in turn, would pay local law enforcement for protection. One of the store owners told Boyles that the district attorney could make a lot of money if he left the liquor business alone.

With the backing of the Department of Justice's head of the Prohibition enforcement division, Mabel Walker Willebrandt, Boyles set in motion plans to snag the city's financial and political elite. Traps were set—eavesdropping, soliciting bribes from dealers, setting up phony liquor operations, even hiring seedy characters to be the front men and make all of this look legit to the wholesalers.

Instead of being a hands-off DA, Boyles actually met with several dealers himself, making them believe that he could easily be on the make himself if the price was right. One of his "front men," Harry French (a man who was under indictment for murder) made connections himself and actually took some bribe money, but instead of turning it over to the federal government, Boyles let French keep it.

On November 13, 1923, Boyles's agents launched a massive raid on warehouses and offices that were "blind tigers" or speakeasies. Truckloads of whiskey were seized and driven to the federal building downtown, where it took workers hours to unload them. The *Mobile Register* reported that twenty-three Mobilians were taken into custody and that the haul of liquor was valued at over $100,000. An agent was quoted as saying, "[I] had never seen such a variety of booze." The headline the following morning declared, "U.S. Men Swoop Down in Liquor Traffic Here."

When the grand jury met on December 15, the indictments that were handed down rocked the city. The list included top Mobile law enforcement men and some of the wealthiest business owners in the city. Included were state representative William Holcombe, his brother Roger, the police chief, a county sheriff, a chief deputy sheriff, the chairman of the county's Democratic Party, attorney Percy Kernes (believed to have been the point person for the wholesalers) and the leader of the liquor trade and one of the city's wealthiest men, Frank W. Boykin. All of those indicted were charged with violating the Volstead Act. Additionally, Boykin and Kerns were also charged with conspiracy to bribe.

When Chief Patrick O'Shaughnessy learned of the indictments, he decided to hop a train bound for New Orleans. When officers caught up with him, O'Shaughnessy told them that he was just "driving around" and thought he'd head to New Orleans for a drink.

At a press conference, Boyles stated that he was offered $150,000 to "slow up" the investigation. After hearing his remarks, District Attorney Bart Chamberlain arrested Boyles on charges of trying to illegally influence two state law enforcement agents. The head of Alabama's Prohibition enforcement department decried the arrest, saying that it was a "gigantic frame-up." Whether it was an attempt to squelch the indictments or not, the pressure was too great, and Boyles had no option but to take a temporary leave of absence from the case until the matter was settled. Boyles was replaced by a future U.S. Supreme Court justice, Birmingham attorney Hugo Black.

The famous Whiskey Trials began on April 3, 1924. Black planned on trying each defendant individually, but after the first trial, that of attorney Percy Kearns, ended in mistrial, Black changed his tactics and went after all of them as a group on a single charge of conspiracy to violate the federal Prohibition law.

The second trial began a few short weeks later on April 28. Boykin was quite the showman during the trail. On the first day of the proceedings, Boykin sauntered into the courtroom considerably late. When Judge W.I.

Grubb asked him where he had been, Boykin coolly responded, "I went to the wrong courtroom." The spectators broke out in raucous laughter. It took the judge some time to get the court back to order.

One of the witnesses for the prosecution, James Daves, was a runner for the wholesalers. He was caught with a huge shipment of liquor by the feds before he could make his delivery.

"I was contacted [by the wholesalers] the other day when I came in from Atlanta," Daves told the court. "I was offered $17,000 not to testify."

"Why didn't you take it?" Black asked.

"I was going to," Daves replied. "I told them I would. I got in my car and was on my way to close the deal a few hours ago."

"What happened?" Black questioned.

Embarrassed, Daves replied, "I ran out of gas."

The trial finally came down to the testimony of Frank Boykin himself, but all he did was deny any involvement. After a short recess, the attorneys made their closing arguments. Following twenty-two hours of deliberation, the jury returned a verdict of not guilty. The judge, however, had something to say about that and announced that Boykin, Holcombe and several others would be brought back into court the following day to stand trial for attempting to bribe federal agents. The key witness would be District Attorney Aubrey Boyles.

Boyles told the court that Boykin promised him that he could make a considerable amount of money if the district attorney would collect taxes on liquor. When asked what his response was, Boyles replied, "I told him I wasn't interested and immediately reported the whole plan to Washington."

When the trial ended, many of the defendants got off with only a stiff fine. Boykin and Holcombe, however, were sentenced to two years in prison plus a fine.

By the end of 1924, state officials reported they had destroyed 1,204,480 bottles of beer, 13,781 gallons of whiskey, 1,754 gallons of wine and 6,587 bottles of home-brew and confiscated 165 cars, 10 trucks, 12 wagons, 9 horses and 7 mules that transported the liquor. When the Twenty-First Amendment to the U.S. Constitution was ratified in 1933, repealing Prohibition, the federal government essentially left it up to states to determine their own laws. The Alabama legislature voted to keep the state dry, with its own prohibition law remaining in effect until 1937. While Alabama's politicians might have believed the state was dry, it was far from that. The Associated Press reported in the final year of Alabama's Bone Dry Law that the state led all others in the number of illegal distilleries captured by the feds.

21

SAFETY FIRST AND OTHER PORT CITY INVENTIONS

T he city of Mobile has had its share of great inventors, men and women who have worked diligently to make the world a better place or, at least, a more fun place. An example of the latter would be the story of Lonnie George Johnson.

Johnson holds a bachelor's degree in mechanical engineering, a master's in nuclear engineering and an honorary doctorate in science from Tuskegee University. His résumé is truly amazing. Johnson has worked with NASA's Jet Propulsion Laboratory in Pasadena, California, and on the Galileo mission to Jupiter, which discovered active volcanoes and a saltwater ocean on one of the planet's moons; he served as the acting chief of the Space Nuclear Power Safety Section of the U.S. Air Force in New Mexico and was even part of NASA's Mars Observer team. And that's only the short list.

You would think that a man of his caliber would be remembered for some lofty discovery in space, but instead, he is known as the man who brought joy to millions of kids—and adults—as the inventor of the Super Soaker.

As with most inventions, the Soaker came out of the blue, and when you think about it, it was quite a simple but ingenious idea. While doing an experiment with a home heat pump, Johnson used water instead of Freon in the unit along with some air pressure.

"I accidentally shot a stream of water across a bathroom where I was doing the experiment," he said. "And I thought to myself, 'This would make a great gun.'"

And with that, the Super Soaker was born. Since its creation, millions have been sold. The toy's sales allowed Johnson to start his own research facility into green technologies, the Johnson Research and Development Company. In 2013, Johnson won a $73 million lawsuit that he brought against the Hasbro Toy Company for failing to pay the agreed upon royalties from 1996 on the toy.

While some inventions, whether accidental or not, result in fun toys for kids, others come from a perceived necessity. One such invention that came from a Mobile-area inventor added to the safety of automobiles. It was the brainchild of Miller Reese Hutchison, a man who would become the right-hand man to one of the country's greatest inventors, Thomas Edison. Over his career, Hutchison patented over one thousand inventions, including the first portable hearing aid and a safety feature for automobiles—the Klaxon Horn.

Hutchison was born on August 6, 1876, in the town of Montrose, which is across from Mobile on Mobile Bay's eastern shore. The son of William and Tracie Hutchison, he attended public school in Mobile, where his interest in mechanics began. From there, he attended Marion Military Institute and Spring Hill College, then ended his education in the Agricultural and Mechanical College at Auburn University, where he graduated in 1897.

Early in his studies, Hutchison became friends with a young man who had greatly reduced hearing due to a bout with scarlet fever. With the knowledge he had been gaining over the years and classes that he took at the Medical College of Alabama to study the anatomy of the human ear, Hutchison created an electrical hearing aid that used a carbon transmitter and electric current to amplify audio sounds. He called the device the Akouphone, and as promised, the young man's hearing was greatly improved.

The only problem was that the device was large, heavy and not portable. It was more of a stationary, tabletop device. In 1902, he patented and sold an updated version, the portable Acousticon. The $400 unit was a huge success and caught the attention of Queen Alexandra of England. Alexandra was fitted with the device, and it was reported that her hearing returned to 90 percent of normal.

Following a tour of duty in the Spanish-American War, Hutchison started his own laboratory, where he devised and patented many other inventions. He moved to New York to be an engineering consultant and married Martha Jackson Pomeroy.

One day, Hutchison was crossing one of the city's notoriously congested and dangerously busy streets during a ferocious rainstorm. Suddenly, a car came out of the rain, but horns on cars of the day were puny and ineffectual, to say the least. With barely a warning, the car came within inches of killing the inventor. It was at that moment that Hutchison came up with an idea for a horn that would be so impactful, so startling, that any pedestrian would be able to hear it and get out of the way in plenty of time. The Klaxon Horn, or as most people know it, the "Ah-Oo-Gah" horn, was born. The word *klaxon* is derived from the Greek word *klaxo*, which means "shriek," and that it did.

The horn was introduced as the Klaxon Warning Signal in *Horseless Age* magazine on January 8, 1908:

> *A new warning device under the above name has been invented by Miller Reese Hutchison of New York and will be manufactured by Lovell McConnell Manufacturing Company of Newark, N.J. It consists simply of a steel diaphragm with a hardened steel pin riveted to it at the centre and a steel cam disc. As the cam disc is revolved, the diaphragm is vibrated violently, which is said to produce a roar "the like of which has never before been heard by man or beast."*

In 1911, Hutchison went to work with Thomas Edison at his laboratory in Menlo Park, New Jersey, where he helped develop a new battery for submarines and went on to become chief engineer at the lab in 1912. When asked about Hutchison, Edison quipped that the young man had created the Klaxon Horn in order to deafen people so that they would have to buy his hearing aids.

Hutchison continued inventing until his death on February 16, 1944.

And then there was the creation of the Mobile Home. No, not pronounced "mo-bull," as in able to be moved from one place to another, but "mo-beel" home, as in "Mobile, Alabama," and it came to us through the craftsmanship and marketing of Laura and James Sweet.

Now, the story that follows has been verified as being true, and although it has been told from generation to generation, some of the details get murky. But still, it's a great story.

The tale begins immediately after the end of World War II, when an economic boon was about to hit the country, especially in the housing market. There was an incredible demand for thousands of new homes across the country for our returning troops. One couple from nearby Prichard, Alabama—Laura and James Sweet—seized on the opportunity.

The couple came up with a design for a prefabricated home that was so light that they could be built at a manufacturing facility, put on a flatbed truck and delivered on site to the customer's property.

The first automobile ads, like this one for a Stearns-Knight, bragged about their accessories, including the Klaxon Horn. *Public domain.*

Their early models were moderately successful, but it was enough to catch the eyes of competitors, who began to flock to the Port City and the South, where they found good, high-quality labor available at a cheap price. With the creation of the interstate highway system by President Dwight D. Eisenhower, the idea caught fire, and a national frenzy took hold, with many dealers and manufacturers sprouting up across the country to build these new portable homes.

Now remember, as I mentioned earlier, the houses were called "Mobile Homes" and named for the town they were built in—Mobile. But as is the case to this day, many people cannot pronounce "Mo-Beel." Instead, they pronounce it "mo-bull," as in being able to transport it across the country, and thus the "mo-bull" home was born.

But this story isn't over yet. In 1951, the couple came up with a catchy radio jingle for an ad that, of course, included the name of their company in it. It was titled "Sweet Homes, Alabama." Later, Lynyrd Skynyrd lifted the tune and reworked it to become the classic "Sweet Home Alabama."

How about a soda to rinse all of this history down with? In 1903, Mobile was going to have its thirst quenched when a new franchise was purchased and opened on Water Street by Walter and William Bellingrath. The franchise was a new Coca-Cola bottling facility that quickly became the nation's most successful. But there was a homegrown competitor in town, and the competition came from French chemist Ed Carre.

Just after the Civil War ended, Carre began a bottling company in downtown Mobile on Franklin Street just north of Dauphin Street, the E. Carre Bottling Company. Carre's company bottled and sold mineral water, cider and soda water. With the introduction of flavors to soda water at the 1876 World's Fair in Philadelphia, the flavored soda market was born, and as the twentieth century rolled in, Carre added to his lineup of drinks. Besides simple fountain water, Carre now offered root beer, cream soda, orange soda and sarsaparilla. He also manufactured his own version of Coca-Cola called Carre Cola.

By this time, there were at least 156 known "versions" of cola drinks across the country, including a second one from Mobile bottled by the Holberg Bottling Works at 315 North Royal Street called Koloko. In 1908, there were growing concerns that these cola products were a health hazard because their key ingredient included an extract from coca leaves—cocaine. A report commissioned by President Theodore Roosevelt said:

The greatest demand is in the South [where] *almost every drug store, confectionery shop and fruit stand has its favorite product on sale. The carbonated goods in bottled form are offered on the trains. People of all classes, young and old, delicate women, and even little children consume these beverages indiscriminately and no warning is ever given of the baneful effect of the powerful habit-forming drugs concealed therein. It is therefore small wonder that the prevalence of the so-called "Coca Cola fiend" is becoming a matter of great importance and concern.*

A two-panel cartoon titled *Baby Killer* appeared in the *Chicago Tribune*. The first panel shows a baby crying in a crib and a mother taking a bottle from a gentleman, with the man saying, "This will stop his crying." The next panel features the mother weeping over an empty crib. Both Carre Cola and Koloko were cited in the government report, while Carre Cola was prominently mentioned in the cartoon's caption. It wouldn't be until 1929 that the process for removing cocaine from the leaves was developed and the drug removed from the soft drinks.

A second Carre product was also listed in the report, but investigators could never determine if the drink ever used coca leaves in its ingredients. It was a grape drink called Fosko.

Carre's bookkeeper, J. Carleton Wilkins Sr. (who would later take over the business in 1918 after Carre's death), hatched the idea of Fosko. The drink was hand mixed in huge cauldrons. Keep in mind that this was during the age of Prohibition, so Carre did some creative marketing. The Fosko motto was "Its winey flavor is great!" Just a subtle hint to consumers during these times.

The drink became a huge success and made the Carre Bottling Company a local favorite, so much so that when the Mobile Bears' new baseball stadium, Hartwell Field, was opened in 1927, Carre was the sole provider of soft drinks in the park. If you bought a bottle of Fosko on the street, it cost a nickel. Inside the park, the price doubled to ten cents a bottle

Wilkins passed away in 1930. His sixteen-year-old son attempted to keep the business going, but the bottling company was forced to close its doors one year later. The family retains the recipe, so maybe, just maybe, one day we can all savor that "winey" taste.

22

THE LEGEND OF HARPO MARX

A s the twentieth century began, when it came to entertainment, choices were limited to say the least. Radio broadcasting as a medium was only a scientific theory, and motion pictures were still in their infancy. There were a few notable exceptions, including the 1902 movie, *Le Voyage dans la Lune* ("A Trip to the Moon") by Georges Méliès and the 1903 western *The Great Train Robbery* by Edwin S. Porter, but the main form of public entertainment for the time was vaudeville.

The word *vaudeville* is believed to have been an anglicized version of the French word *vaux-de-vire*, which was a form of satirizing popular songs in the fifteenth century. In the United States, vaudeville became recognized as a form of light entertainment consisting of ten to fifteen unrelated acts. Producers would organize the shows with a contingent of singers, dancers, magicians, acrobats, jugglers and, most notably, comedians, to tour the country in what became known as "the circuit."

Between 1850 and the early 1930s, vaudeville spawned a great number of comedians who would later go on to adapt to the new forms of media that were developing—motion pictures, radio, even television. Some of these vaudevillians included W.C. Fields, Jack Benny, Burns and Allen, Red Skelton and the irreverent humor of the Marx Brothers.

After seeing the success of their uncle Al Sheen on the vaudeville circuit, Minnie Marx, the Marx Brothers' aunt, believed that the siblings could be just as popular on the stage as Sheen. In 1909, Minnie and the boys put together an act that they called *Minnie Marx and her Four Nightingales*.

In 1910, Minnie added the brothers' aunt Hannah to the act, renaming the troupe Minnie Palmer's Six Mascots. That year proved to be an important one for the Marx Brothers and for one of them in particular, Adolph Marx, later to be known as Harpo.

That year, Minnie and the boys found themselves on a grueling tour that saw them perform thirty shows a week in venues scattered across every conceivable corner of the country: Gadsden, Alabama; Little Rock, Arkansas; St. Joseph, Missouri; Muskogee, Oklahoma; Laredo, Texas; Youngstown, Ohio; Rockford, Illinois; Butte, Montana; Elko, Nevada; San Francisco, California; Fargo, North Dakota; Chicago, Illinois; and Mobile, Alabama.

Following a performance of their comedy sketch *Fun in Hi Skule* in Champaign, Illinois, a critic for the Champaign-Urbana newspaper wrote that "the Marx Brother who plays [the character of] 'Patsy Brannigan' is made up and costumed to a fare-thee-well and he takes off on an Irish immigrant most amusingly in pantomime. Unfortunately, the effect is spoiled when he speaks."

In his book *Harpo Speaks!*, Adolph said he was devastated. He realized that he couldn't outtalk his brother Groucho. At that moment, he vowed to his aunt Minnie that he would never "utter another word, onstage or in front of a camera as a Marx Brother."

Minnie didn't try to change his mind, and the rest is history.

For a time, the act was barely getting by. The brothers weren't a total failure, but they weren't burning up the vaudeville circuit, either. They began looking for a way to add something new and creative to the act, something no one else had tried. One day while in Aurora, Illinois, Adolph received a telegram from Minnie that read:

DON'T LEAVE TOWN UNTIL YOUR SHIPMENT ARRIVES BY FREIGHT. PAYMENTS ON IT: ONE DOLLAR PER WEEK. DON'T GET IT WET.

Adolph wondered what it could be. A unicycle? A dog? It was none of the above. It was a harp. Minnie had put forty-five dollars down on the instrument, and Adolph was to make the weekly installment payment of one dollar a week.

Not knowing how to play, he went about learning the old-fashioned way—hunting and pecking until he finally learned the song "Annie Laurie." When he first played the song on stage before an audience in Gadsden, Alabama, the crowd was so impressed that they demanded an encore. The

A theater card from the Marx Brothers' third motion picture, *Monkey Business*. *Public domain.*

only song he knew was "Annie Laurie," so he played it again. The making of Harpo Marx was complete. According to Harpo, the mere appearance of the harp alone—not the harpist—raised their monthly salary by five dollars a month.

During that same tour in 1910, as they made their way by train in the early morning hours from Gadsden to Mobile by way of Montgomery, the passengers were startled awake by what was described as "one hell of a jolt." The train had derailed, and while the main Pullman car where the bulk of the passengers slept was OK, the forward coach for people of color and the baggage car were destroyed. People were crying out in pain, and the brothers pitched in to help tend to wounds of the suffering wherever they could.

It wasn't long before insurance adjusters were on the scene making passengers sign release waivers that gave each of them a paltry settlement—one dollar for a bad bruise, two dollars for gashed face, five dollars for a broken arm and ten dollars for a broken leg.

Harpo raced to the baggage car to find that the case for his harp had been destroyed, but the instrument inside was intact and barely had even a scratch on it. He saw his chance to upgrade to a more expensive harp and he threw the instrument off the train and onto the tracks, breaking it to pieces.

When the insurance adjusters came by, he told them the harp cost forty-five dollars. The adjuster said, "The rule is 50 percent, but you look like a nice fellow. I'll pay you twenty-five."

Minnie was incensed and shouted, "You don't pull that on us! We're getting a lawyer!"

The adjuster just replied, "Damn Yankees."

The family headed on to Mobile, where they found an attorney who quickly forced the railroad company to make immediate reparations. When it was over, Harpo received $200 for his old $45 harp and bought his first "really good" harp. On that day, he vowed that he would learn how to play it correctly, learn other keys to play in besides E flat, learn how to tune it and would never, *ever*, take it for a ride in a Model T Ford.

23

MOBILE IS ON THE AIR!

The year was 1929. On October 29, the worst stock market crash in history rattled Wall Street, sending shock waves across the country. Black Tuesday, as it was called, saw stockholders lose over $40 billion. With the crash came a gripping fear among Americans that the economy was going to get worse, so they began purchasing less, which meant a rapid slowdown in production in the manufacturing sector and led to massive layoffs—a domino effect.

To make matters worse, in the West and Midwest, a severe drought turned once fertile and fruitful farmland into nothing more than a giant dust bowl.

Things were not much better along the Gulf Coast. With production being cut across the country and heavy taxes levied on imports, the Port of Mobile saw a drastic reduction in shipping down 40 percent. Retail sales shrank by $10 million; 10 percent of all adults in the city went on some form of monetary relief. Teachers were being paid with IOUs in the belief that they would be repaid in full once the crisis was over. People couldn't afford to pay doctors, so instead they offered them food or labor as payment.

Times were tough, and the city needed a pick-me-up, something to help residents forget their worries and at the same time inform them about the news of the world. Even though radio broadcasting had been established almost ten years earlier in 1920 with the first broadcast over KDKA in Pittsburgh, in 1929, Mobile was lagging well behind the rest of the country in the new technology. Getting news in the Port City was limited to its retelling by sailors who arrived on steamers at the waterfront, tourists who frequented the city or by listening to radio stations farther away in Montgomery or even WCOA in Pensacola, Florida. But that would all change the following year.

Enter Frederick I. Thompson.

Frederick I. Thompson was a newspaperman through and through. He began his career in journalism at an early age, becoming the editor of the *Aberdeen Weekly* in Mississippi at the age of seventeen. At age twenty, he left the paper and moved to Memphis, where he became the editor of the *Commercial Appeal.* It is also where he met his future wife, Adrianna Ingate, who hailed from Mobile.

After stints with a few other papers, he arrived in Mobile in 1910 and became the chief owner and publisher of the *Mobile Daily* and the *Sunday Register.* Six years later, he bought the competing *Mobile News Item.*

In 1930, Thompson partnered with Hunter Watkins and William Pape to bring the first radio station to Mobile. The station broadcast on a frequency of 1410 on the AM band and provided the much needed and sought-after entertainment and news from not only around the city but around the world as well. Thompson envisioned the station's programming to be light entertainment, something that the public could turn on and relax with to forget their troubles.

One of the first public notices of the partners' grand plan appeared in the *Mobile Register* on January 12, 1930. The piece featured a simple photo of the new station's transmitter site and antenna tower on the west side of town on Moffat Road. An inset photo featured the image of the station's first chief engineer, a stogy-wielding former Coast Guard electrical engineer, A.P. Arlington.

On February 1, the station officially announced its schedule for opening night, February 7. The headline in the paper proudly announced, "'On Mobile Bay' will Herald W.O.D.X. from the Register, News-Item Studio." The article then went on to list the station's programming for the night in minute-by-minute detail:

> *8:00 Opening announcement by announcer Al Treadway (musical background of "On Mobile Bay")*
> *8:03 Studio Orchestra, "On Mobile Bay"*
> *8:06 Dedication of station, by Hunter Watkins*
> *8:10 Reply to dedication, by Mayor Harry T. Hartwell*
> *8:15 Studio Orchestra*
> *8:18 Address*
>
> *…*
>
> *8:45 "Mobile Under Five Flags," a historical sketch with chorus and orchestra*

The list went on and on, highlighting just about every city and county commissioner, auto club and garden club that would be sending greetings to not only Mobile but also the entire Southeast over the airwaves that night, all interspersed with an eclectic assortment of performers, including the Kiwanis Glee Club, a piano novelty played by Mrs. Paul Pirtle, a soprano solo by singer Lucille Ravier, Nelstone's Hawaiian Strings, blind musician George Tremer and, at 2:00 a.m., when the station would shut down for the night, the singing of the song "Good Night" by Al and Eloise.

Local shops began to prepare for the broadcast as well, buying up advertising in the *Register* to promote the latest Atwater Kent radio, which had arrived in stores just in time for opening night. Greer's grocery store advertised that shoppers could have the opportunity to hear their favorite musical selections sung and performed by the Kiwanis Glee Club and the Greer's "Rattling Good Instrumental Ensemble" live on the air. Simply write the request on a piece of paper and drop it by Store No. 30 at the corner of St. Louis and Bayou Streets.

The stage was set. Just before 8:00 p.m. on February 7, the tubes in the WODX transmitter lit up and began to hum. Mobile was on the air! The studio was packed with people. Not only were the advertised dignitaries in

The WODX Studio Band getting ready to take to the air. *Mobile Public Library Digital Collections.*

attendance during this first broadcast, but it was reported that hundreds of Mobilians showed up throughout the night as well, with each and every one being greeted by the co-owners, Watkins and Pape.

In the opening remarks, Mayor Hartwell summed up the moment quite nicely when he said, "We are no longer 'Old Mobile.' It is true that we are preserving much of our history and many of our old landmarks, but, at the same time, we are blending with the old traditions the new tonight."

The following morning, the headline in the *Register* blared in big, bold font, "Mobile's First Night on Air Great Success!" The morning's editorial cartoon depicted WODX's twin radio towers broadcasting the "Winged Words of Mobile" to the world.

Thousands of telegrams were received from as far away as Chicago, congratulating the city on the great opening night programming. Alabama governor Bibb Graves was one of the first to telegram the studios:

> *I am delighted the city of Mobile has availed itself of the opportunities of expression and of bringing itself into closer contact with the outside world afforded by the radio.*

One local listener suggested that the call letters should stand for "Where Old Dixie eXports," a name that stuck with listeners.

From that opening night broadcast, the station began to expand its programming. An interesting feature that first appeared on February 14, 1930, was a series of programs hosted by a Mobile historian, the self-proclaimed "Old Narrator," John F. Glennon. On the first show, Glennon gave his audience a broad, sweeping overview of the history of Mobile. Each week, he delved deeper into the city's history, telling stories of the *Hunley* (the first operational submarine built in Mobile), the early French and Spanish colonists and more. The show was wildly popular and was quickly bumped up from one night a week to three.

In 1933, the station was sold, and its new owners were granted a call letter change by the FCC from WODX to WALA. Thompson went on to have continued success in both business and politics. He was appointed to the Advisory Board of Public Works by President Franklin Roosevelt, attained a position on the Alabama State Docks Commission and became president of the Seaboard Investment Company. And Thompson's involvement in broadcasting wasn't quite over yet. On April 8, 1939, he became the director of the Federal Communications Commission.

Thompson passed away in Mobile on February 20, 1952.

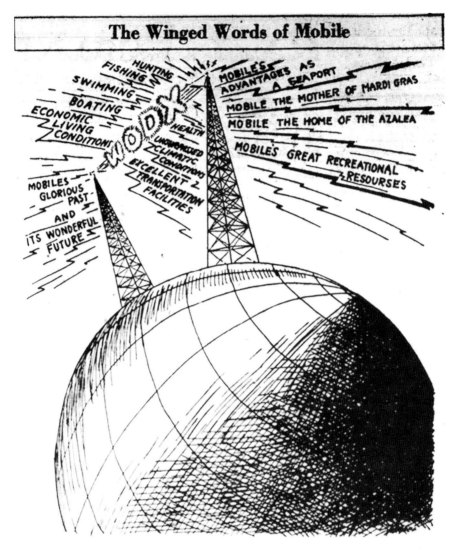

This *Mobile Register* editorial cartoon has nothing but glowing praise for WODX's opening night on the air. *Mobile Public Library Local History & Genealogy.*

Since that time, the frequency 1410AM has undergone many owner and call letter changes. The first was the change to WALA, which from all appearances looks like it's an abbreviation for "Alabama." Then it became WUNI which stood for "You and I" but was pronounced "Woonie." The station had a weird little bird, the "Woonie Bird," as its mascot. From WUNI it became WMML, which was named for its new owner, stuttering country singer M-m-el Tillis, only to be changed again to WLVV ("Love Radio") and finally, WNGL (Arch "Angel" radio).

No matter what the station format has been or its call letters, the frequency 1410AM in Mobile will always be a lasting memory of days gone by and the Port City's first radio station, WODX.

24

IT MUST BE THE WATER

Baseball has always been an important part of life in Mobile. On any given day, the thick, humid air of summer is pierced by the shouts of young boys and girls playing on a local diamond. The game came ashore with sailors in the mid-nineteenth century and quickly grew roots here, creating some of the greats of the game.

The history of the game in Mobile can be traced as far back as 1860, when Alabama's Jesuit college, Springhill, fielded a team—the Springhill Badgers. Over the years, the Badgers played exhibition games with some impressive teams like the 1909 Chicago Cubs and were schooled on hitting home runs by the "Sultan of Swat," Babe Ruth.

As recounted in my book *Baseball in Mobile*, it was at this time that the Azalea City sparked what would become the phenomenal baseball craze on the island of Cuba that continues to this very day. In 1860, a young man from Havana enrolled at Springhill College. His name was Nemisio Guillo. Upon graduation in 1864, Guillo returned to Cuba, bringing with him the first balls and bats. In 1878, Guillo organized the first- ever team on the island, Club Habana. In the first official game in Cuban baseball history, Guillo's Club Habana defeated a newly formed team, Club Matanzas, by an incredible score of 51 to 9.

Soon after, Guillo organized the island's first league, the Cuban Professional League, where his Club Habana team won the first six league championships.

Mobile had started the baseball craze in Cuba.

The Port City fielded its first professional teams—Acid Iron Earth (which was named for a popular local cure-all elixir of the day) and

Club Mobile—in 1886. Those two teams, as well as two teams from New Orleans—the Robert E. Lees and Club New Orleans—were part of a new four-team league, the Gulf Baseball League.

Even at this early stage, baseball wasn't a whites-only sport. Long before the advent of the famed Negro League with standout players from Mobile such as Ted "Double Duty" Radcliff, "Showboat" Thomas and the "Human Vacuum" Bobby Robinson, black teams were taking to the field at Frascati Park on Mobile's Cedar Point against teams from New Orleans.

Since those early days, Mobile has either produced many outstanding homegrown major-league players or has been the breeding ground for successful players after playing on one of the city's minor-league teams. The most famous of those born in Mobile are the city's five Hall of Fame players—Billy Williams, Ozzie Smith, Willie McCovey, Satchel Paige and the one and only "Hammerin'" Hank Aaron. The induction of these players into the Baseball Hall of Fame places Mobile third on the list of cities that have produced the most Hall of Famers.

From there the list goes on and on—the "Mets from Mobile": Tommy Agee, Cleon Jones and Amos Otis; Hank's brother Tommie Aaron; Boston's Dave Stapleton; the Bolling brothers, Milt and Frank, just to name a few. And then there are those who passed through the city, cutting their teeth on the game by playing on one of Mobile's minor-league teams: Don Zimmer, George "Shotgun" Shuba, Chris Kitsos, Luis Gonzales, Mike Mordecai, even future TV star Chuck Connors, the "Rifleman," played ball in Mobile.

It got to the point that so many players were coming out of Mobile and making a name for themselves in the big leagues that Hank Aaron was asked what he attributed the phenomena to. His reply? "It must be the water."

There are some names, however, that need to share the spotlight with the greats mentioned above. They were standouts in their own right, doing something that no other ball players from the city had done: the first player from Mobile and the entire state of Alabama to hit the big leagues, Charlie Edward "Home Run" Duffee, and Mobile's own girls of the All-American Girls Professional Baseball League, Margaret "Marge" Holgerson Silvestri and Delores "Dolly" Brumfield White.

Charlie Duffee was born in Mobile on January 27, 1866. Not much is known about his early life in the Port City until his name appears on the roster of Mobile's first professional team, Acid Iron Earth, in 1886. He began his career as the lead-off hitter because of his smallish size of five feet, five inches tall, but the following year, after hitting six home runs, they moved him to the middle of the lineup and he became known as Charlie "Home Run" Duffee.

From there, Duffee bounced between teams in the newly formed Southern League, first signing with the Birmingham Ironmakers, then coming back to Mobile to play with the Swamp Angels, then back to Birmingham with the Maroons. He also did a brief stint on the New Orleans Pelicans of the Texas-Southern League.

In 1889, a new major league was formed to give the National League a run for its money—the American Association (not to be confused with the American League, which was established years later). The league was affectionately nicknamed the "Beer and Whiskey League" due to the fact that it offered something the National League didn't—games on Sunday and alcohol.

This was Duffee's big break. He signed on to play with the St. Louis Browns (now known as the St. Louis Cardinals). His debut came on April 17, 1889, in a 5–0 win over the Cincinnati Red Stockings, making him the first Mobilian—and Alabamian—to play in the big leagues.

The outfielder played in 137 games that year and posted some pretty strong numbers: .244 batting average with 124 hits, 93 runs, 86 runs batted in and 21 stolen bases. Duffee lived up to his "Home Run" nickname that season, as he banged out 16 home runs, a record at the time for batters with a batting average less than .250

While with the Browns, Duffee and his team faced the formidable Brooklyn Bridegrooms (later to be known as the Brooklyn Dodgers). Brooklyn fans were known for their fanatical behavior toward their team, and one game saw the Browns actually fear for their own safety. After leaving the city, Duffee was quoted as saying, "I would rather hoe cotton down in Alabama for ten dollars a month than run the gauntlet of Brooklyn fans!"

Duffee missed the first two months of the 1890 season with St. Louis due to an illness that kept him bedridden

OLD JUDGE CIGARETTES Goodwin & Co., New York.

There had to be a first. Charlie Duffee was the first pro baseball player not only from Mobile but also from Alabama. *Library of Congress Prints and Photographs Division.*

at his home in Mobile. When he returned, a poor performance forced the Browns to trade him to the Columbus Solons in the postseason.

Unfortunately, even with beer sales at ballparks and Sunday games, the American Association began experiencing financial difficulties, and by the end of the 1891 season, the league had dissolved. In that final season with Columbus, Duffee and the Solons played in the first major-league game played in Minnesota.

Up to this point, the Milwaukee Brewers had played only away games and not a single game at home. Now, with the league getting ready to fold, they relocated to Minneapolis, Minnesota, to play out the season against the Solons. The *St. Paul Pioneer Press* said, "Having lost all prestige in their own towns the two teams sought to run up to Minneapolis and replenish their exchequers."

Columbus fell to the Brewers by a score of 5–0 on October 2, 1891, making this game the first to be played in Minnesota and the last until 1961. The final game of the season was postponed because of weather, but the two would meet again, this time back in Milwaukee, where the Brewers won 8–4.

In 1892, the American Association closed its doors for good, with most of the teams being absorbed by the National League, raising its number of franchises to twelve. This expansion of the league inspired the phrase "big league." Columbus wasn't one of those teams taken in by the National League, but Duffee—who was now playing short stop—managed to survive by being picked up by the Washington Senators.

In 1893, at the age of twenty-seven, he was traded once again to the Cincinnati Red Stockings, where he would only play four games. This short stint with the Reds proved to be the end of Duffee's major-league career. He did finish out the season on the playing field, playing outfield and third base in sixty-eight games for the Southern Association's minor-league team, the Atlanta Windjammers. In August, the *Atlanta Constitution* wrote that "Duffee's health is not very good, and he has gone to his home in Mobile."

Duffee did indeed return home to Mobile, working for a short time at a saloon, but it wasn't long before he was confined to bed. On Christmas Eve 1894, Charlie "Home Run" Duffee passed away, succumbing to tuberculosis.

Who doesn't love the movie *A League of Their Own*? It's the story of the Rockford Peaches and the players of the All-American Girls Professional Baseball League (AAGPBL). The 1992 Penny Marshall–directed movie stars Tom Hanks, Geena Davis, Madonna and Rosie O'Donnell and tells the story of two sisters who start out as teammates in a brand-new all-girl baseball league but soon become rivals on opposing teams.

Up until the release of the movie, most Americans didn't realize that there really was an AAGPBL, but there was, and two of the area's own were a part of it: Margaret "Marge" Holgerson Silvestri and Delores "Dolly" Brumfield White.

As World War II engulfed the world, the commitment of manpower in the United States to fight the war was enormous. Manufacturing was hardest hit by the loss of male workers, so much so that women were called on to man the machinery that would build the arms needed to win the war. Even Major League Baseball was feeling the pinch, with many teams in smaller cities being forced to shut down due to the lack of male players.

Realizing that there was a wealth of talented female ball players out there, the owner of the Chicago Cubs, Phillip Wrigley, formed the All-American Girls Professional Baseball League in 1943. The league became a hit.

Three years later in Mobile, nineteen-year old Marge Holgerson took a gamble and tried out to become a player in the league. She impressed the scouts, handily made the cut and was assigned to play with the Rockford Peaches in 1946.

Holgerson had a standout rookie season with the Peaches. She began playing second base, but it wasn't long before the team's manager, Bill Allington, realized that she had a natural sidearm delivery, which is how the league required the girls to pitch at the time, and switched her to the pitcher's mound. In that first season, the right hander pitched thirty-three innings in five starts, allowing only seven runs and recorded eight strikeouts.

At about the same time, just north of Mobile in the neighboring town of Prichard, a young woman who identified herself as a tomboy was embracing the game as well, Delores Brumfield.

On any given afternoon, you could find Delores playing in a pickup game of ball near her school. Since there wasn't a girls' team in town, she would watch the games being played by shipyard workers in Mobile's industrial league. When the men needed someone to fill in, they would have the then thirteen-year-old girl step up to the plate.

It was March 1946 when the shipyard workers heard that the AAGPBL was holding tryouts in nearby Pascagoula, Mississippi. They persuaded Delores to try out. Delores's mother, however, was not sold on the idea of her little girl playing baseball and not keen at all of her little girl hitching a ride with the shipyard workers to the tryout. So her mom borrowed her grandmother's car, took her out of school for the day and drove her to the tryouts.

The young teen impressed league president Max Carey, but there was one problem—she was too young. So Delores went back to Mobile and began playing on the Brookley Air Force Base softball team. The following year, a letter arrived at the Brumfield house. It was from Max Carey asking Delores's parents if they would allow her to attend the AAGPBL spring training camp in Havana.

With the assurance that each girl would be accompanied by a chaperone and mentor, her parents reluctantly agreed and sent her off to Cuba. For Delores, the chaperone assigned to her was Marge Holgerson.

Delores recalls that this was the highlight of her career—the chance to meet girls from all over North America and Cuba. She remembers that her thick southern drawl was difficult for Yankees to understand, but in the end, Delores, now fourteen years old, was selected to play for the South Bend Blue Sox, making her the youngest player in the league and earning her fifty-five dollars a week. With the new team came a new chaperone, an older married player, Daisy Junior, who began calling Delores "Dolly." The nickname stuck.

Considering Dolly was only fourteen at the time, she did pretty well for herself that first season with a batting average of .117 and 15 walks in only 103 at-bats, and when she got on base, she stole six bases.

That 1947 season was a big year for Dolly's former chaperone, Marge Holgerson, both on and off the field. On the field, her earned run average (ERA) was 2.42 with 48 strikeouts in 201 innings. Off the field, she married and began playing the game under her married name, Silvestri.

Things changed the following year, not only for Marge, but for all pitchers in the league, as the league changed to overhand throws instead of sidearm. This was a boon for the young pitcher. Her ERA dropped to 1.92, sixth lowest in the league, and she finished fourth that year with the most strikeouts. The icing on the cake was when the Peaches defeated the Fort Wayne Daisies in the best of five championship series.

Meanwhile, Dolly was doing a balancing act, juggling baseball with high school. For the next three years, during the off season, she attended Murphy High School, and inevitably, she would miss the last classes in the spring due to having to report to training camp. Then in the fall, she would start school well after everyone else due to a long season. But even with all of this, she managed to graduate from Murphy in 1948.

Holgerson's career was split in both the 1949 and 1950 seasons between two teams. The year 1949 saw her start the season with Rockford, but she was then traded midseason to the Muskegon Lassies. The following year, she began with Muskegon and finished the season with the Grand Rapids Chicks. Her playing career ended in 1952 with Grand Rapids, the same year that the All-American Girls Professional Baseball League closed down.

Dolly saw a few changes in teams as well, moving from the Blue Sox to the Kenosha Comets in 1948; she had her best season in 1951, raising her batting average to 2.73. In 1952, Dolly was traded to the Fort Wayne Daisies under manager Jimmie Foxx. Foxx was a Hall of Fame player and the inspiration for the Tom Hank's character Jimmy Dugen in the movie. Dolly recalls that in one game, Foxx told her quite matter-of-factly that she was going to play second base.

"Second base?" she said. "I never played second base!"

Foxx just plainly replied, "That's OK."

End of discussion.

Fort Wayne won the championship that year, but Dolly missed the playoffs after breaking her ankle in a collision with a catcher at the plate.

With dwindling attendance and baseball back on track to be America's pastime, the All-American Girls Professional Baseball League ended operations in 1954. For Marge, her career ended with a record of 76 wins, 69 loses and 599 strikeouts, placing her as one of the league's top-ten best pitchers. Marge returned to Mobile but didn't quite give up the game. She acted as umpire in both men's and women's leagues throughout the area.

On March 23, 1990, Marge Holgerson Silvestri passed away at age sixty-three.

Dolly was twenty-one years old when the league dissolved. With lack of encouragement from her parents, but the full support of her friends and teammates, she took the money she had earned from playing ball and enrolled at the Alabama College for Women (now known as the University of Montevallo), where she earned her degree in physical education.

She continued her education, earning a master's degree in 1959 and a doctorate in 1969 from the University of South Mississippi in physical education. She began teaching at Henderson State University in Arkadelphia, Arkansas, where she met and married her husband, Joe White, in 1977. Dolly retired in 1994 and was presented with the title professor emeritus.

Dolly remains deeply involved and committed to advancing the cause of sports, not only baseball but all sports, for both men and most especially women.

In a 2011 interview with *Mobile Bay Magazine*, Dolly said, "I think that we, as young women baseball players all those years ago, sort of forged the way for girls today to be able to do the things they do. It makes me really proud to know that I had a part in making it easier for women to be involved in sports."

Delores "Dolly" Brumfield White was inducted into the Mobile Sports Hall of Fame in 2011.

25

ELVIS, THE RADIO RANCH AND VIGOR HIGH

The "King of Rock 'n' Roll," Elvis Aaron Presley, visited Mobile many times before his death in 1977. How many of you Mobilians still remember his last concert in the city at what was then called the Municipal Auditorium (now known as the Mobile Civic Center)?

Elvis was originally scheduled to appear there on April 1, 1977, but he was forced to cancel due to being hospitalized with intestinal flu. He rescheduled the show for June 2, and that night, with blaring trumpets and a heavily sequined outfit that he called the "Mexican Sundial," the King rocked the auditorium before a sell-out crowd.

Two months later, Elvis was dead.

The story of Elvis in Mobile begins many years before, back before he was the leader of the worldwide rock 'n' roll revolution that swept the country and the world. Back when he would drive from town to town with his band mates Bill Black, Scotty Moore and D.J. Fontana, visiting local radio stations to plug their latest record and to make appearances at local dives, night clubs and county fairs, they would even play local high schools, including one in Mobile—Vigor High School.

The Tupelo, Mississippi rocker first stepped into a recording studio in July 1953 to record several demos, including "My Happiness" and "That's When Your Heartache Begins." For some time, the band toured exclusively around the north Mississippi area, but as Elvis's popularity slowly grew, he began branching out to play more gigs outside of Mississippi in Tennessee, Arkansas, Alabama and Texas.

Elvis's big break came on July 5, 1954, when he recorded his first hit single, "That's All Right, Mama," for RCA. He was on the cusp of breaking the rock world wide open. As his career began to pick up steam, the band began crisscrossing the country as an opening act for bigger name entertainers and started playing larger venues.

The following year saw Elvis come to Mobile on several occasions. He still wasn't the King, not quite yet, but he was getting close. His first appearance that year in the Port City was as an act on country singer Hank Snow's *Jamboree Show*. For two nights, May 4 and 5, Mobile's Ladd Stadium was the *Jamboree*'s fourth stop on its three-week tour. The *Mobile Register* ran a short column on the event, with a bold headline reading, "2 Music Shows Slated at Ladd," then went on to flesh out the lineup with Elvis and his "sidekicks" at the bottom of the bill:

> *Two straight nights of country-style music, featuring Hank Snow and 25 recording artists, will begin Wednesday at Ladd Stadium. Show time both nights is 8:15 pm., with stadium gates to be opened at 7. Each two-hour session will feature western and country style music, together with hymns and novelty numbers. Besides Snow and his Rainbow Ranch Boys, the program also lists Faron Young and the Wilburn Brothers, Mother Maybelle and the Carter Sisters, Jimmy Rodgers Snow (Hank's young son), the Davis Sisters, and Onie Wheeler—all of Grand Ole Opry fame. Elvis Presley, with his sidekicks Bill and Scotty, will be here from the Louisiana Hayride. Tickets are now on sale at Walgreen's in Mobile, and at McMillan No. 1 and 2, Prichard.*

To help promote the show, young Elvis fans were encouraged to stop by the Prichard Music and Appliance Store to get a free autographed photo of Elvis when they bought one of his RCA Victor singles.

By this time, Elvis was beginning to become the heartthrob of girls across the country, and they were becoming a little obsessive. Years later, Snow's son, Jimmy Rodgers Snow, recalled that during the Ladd Stadium show, Elvis was chased by a swarm of girls across the stadium's football field.

Later during his visit, Elvis and his mates stopped at a local burger joint—Johnny's Drive-In, your quintessential drive in hamburger and malt shop—located at the loop in midtown Mobile. Frenzied girls hopped out of their cars in hopes of getting a glimpse of the rocker. The diner's owner, Johnny Vallas, said that he had to "run [Elvis] out of the parking lot because there were too many people out of their cars!"

Speaking of eating, Elvis also loved to dine at the famous Bluegill Restaurant on the Causeway that connects Mobile to the eastern shore of Mobile Bay. If you visit the restaurant today, you will see a plaque at booth 24, his special seat.

Elvis would come back to Mobile again in 1955 to play several venues, including the largest nightclub in Mobile, Curtis Gordon's Radio Ranch.

Curtis Gordon was born and raised in Moultrie, Georgia. Like many young men of the day in the South, he loved singing country music, especially western swing, and was often heard over the Moultrie radio station WMGA.

He moved to Biloxi, Mississippi, in the late 1940s and played with Pee Wee Mills and his Twilight Playboys until 1949 when he left the group to start his own band, the Circle A Wranglers. Three years later, the band won a talent contest in Atlanta and a recording contract with RCA Victor Records.

During this time, Gordon—now with the nickname "Mr. Personality"—released several popular country singles for RCA, including "The Greatest Sin" and "I Just Don't Love You Anymore." He toured the Southeast extensively to promote his recordings before he finally made his way to Mobile, where he appeared for thirteen weeks on Mobile's *Dixie Barn Dance* radio show, which aired over WKAB radio.

While his career wasn't a blockbuster, he was still making a decent living, but the music world was changing and so was Curtis Gordon. He was moving away from country ballads to the harder rockabilly sound that was beginning to sweep the nation. RCA terminated his contract in 1954, but he was immediately picked up by Mercury Records and given virtually free rein over his career, recording some rockin' rockabilly tunes, including an homage to his "new" hometown, titled appropriately enough, "Mobile, Alabama."

Apparently, Gordon loved the Port City and decided to give the folks of Mobile a place where they could hear "the best music around." Along a stretch of Cedar Point Road in south Mobile, just off of Dauphin Island Parkway, he built what was billed as "Mobile's largest nightclub"—the Radio Ranch.

At this point, his career was doing well and so was the Radio Ranch, with people coming in from across the region to hear some of the big names in country and rockabilly music. A local favorite that played the club regularly was the former pedal steel player for Pee Wee King's band and the host of the highly popular show on Mobile's WKRG-TV, the *Alabama Jubilee*, Don Davis. More nationally recognized artists appearing at the club included Jerry Lee Lewis and Elvis.

An ad that appeared in the *Mobile Register* for Elvis Presley's shows at the Radio Ranch Nightclub at Cedar Point. *Mobile Public Library Local History & Genealogy.*

Elvis played the Radio Ranch at least three times in 1955, doing two shows on June 29 and 30, performing again in October. It was during this October visit that—as hard as it is to believe—the King of Rock 'n' Roll performed at an assembly of high school students. The performance would be at Vigor High School.

To the north of Mobile is the small town of Prichard, Alabama. In 1955, Prichard was a bustling suburb of Mobile, with shoppers flocking to the many shops that lined its main thoroughfare. The town's high school, Vigor High, was only eleven years old at the time and its auditorium only three years old when the King rocked its halls.

It was October 28, 1955, when Elvis came back to town for performances at the Radio Ranch and Greater Gulf State Fair. A local radio station booked him to play for the students at the high school. Now you would think that by this time Elvis would be playing much larger venues, but as odd as it sounds, he would quite often play high schools in these early years. In fact, he had just played at a high school in Ohio the day before.

In an interview with ScottyMoore.Net, then Vigor ninth grader Margaret Williams Burcham remembered the performance. "I remember the auditorium was full. We loved assembly programs because we got out of class. We had over 330 in my graduating class so I know the auditorium held many more than that."

Elvis, Bill and Scotty were introduced, and at 10:00 a.m., the show began. Elvis belted out tune after tune, his legendary hips gyrating with the music. The principal, J.M. Laird, was "disgusted" by the carnal gyrations. Throughout the show, Elvis joked with the kids between songs—that is, until one joke shut it all down: "What happened to the farmer who was milking the cow that jumped over the moon? He was left holding the bag."

The students roared with laughter, and one of the school's teachers reported it to the principal, who then shut the show down. The entire performance lasted thirty minutes and ended with students storming out of the auditorium.

Elvis went on to become one of the biggest superstars in music history. Curtis Gordon sold the radio ranch in 1959, but the building was destroyed by fire a few years later and never rebuilt. Gordon passed away in 2004 at the age of seventy-five.

And as far as we know, there has never been another rock 'n' roll performer of that magnitude to be invited to play at a Mobile area high school. Not after Elvis.

BIBLIOGRAPHY

Book References

Atkins, Ronald. *All That Jazz: The Illustrated Story of Jazz Music.* London: Carlton Books Limited, 1996.

Badger, Reid. *A Life in Ragtime.* Oxford, UK: Oxford University Press, 1995.

Bergeron, Arthur, Jr. *Confederate Mobile.* Baton Rouge: Louisiana State University Press, 1991.

Bivens, Shawn A. *Mobile, Alabama's People of Color: A Tri-centennial History, 1702–2002.* Vol. 1. Victoria, BC: Trafford Publishing, 2004.

Brunson, James E., III. *Black Baseball, 1858–1900: A Comprehensive Record of All Teams, Players, Managers, Owners, and Umpires.* Jefferson, NC: McFarland, 2015.

Butler, Ruth Lapham. *Journal of Paul du Ru, February 1 to May 8, 1700, Missionary Priest to Louisiana.* Chicago: Caxton Club, 1934.

Carmer, Carl. *Stars Fell on Alabama.* New York: Farrar and Reinhart, 1934.

Cuhaj, Joe, and Tamra Carraway-Hinckle. *Baseball in Mobile.* Charleston, SC: Arcadia Publishing, 2004.

Décharné, Max. *A Rocket in My Pocket: A Hipster's Guide to Rockabilly.* London: Serpent's Tail, 2010.

Flannery, Gerald V. *Commissioners of the FCC: 1927–1994.* Lanham, MD: University Press of America, 1995.

Forsman, Creighton C. *She's Bound to Be a Goer: Fairhope, Alabama and the Steamboats of Mobile.* Silverhill, AL: Creekhouse Publishing, 2014.

Friend, Jack. *West Wind, Flood Tide: The Battle of Mobile Bay.* Annapolis, MD: Naval Institute Press, 2004.

Glennon, Robert McNeil. *Alabama History on the Air! Mobile's Radio Broadcasts of the 1930s.* Fairhope, AL: Nall Printing, 2009.

Green, Hilary. *Educational Reconstruction: African American Schools in the Urban South, 1865–1890.* New York: Fordham University Press, 2016.

Hamilton, Peter J. *The Charter and the Code of Ordinances of 1897 of the City of Mobile, with an Appendix.* Mobile, AL: Commercial Printing Company, 1897.

———. *Colonial Mobile: An Historical Study Largely from Original Sources, of the Alabama-Tombigbee Basin and South West, from the Discovery of the Spiritu Santo in 1519 until the Demolition of Fort Charlotte in 1821.* Boston: Houghton, Mifflin and Company, 1898.

———. *Mobile of the Five Flags: The Story of the River Basin and Coast About Mobile from Earliest Times to Present.* Mobile, AL: Gill Printing Company, 1913.

Hammond, Elizabeth. *Modern Domestic Cookery and Useful Recipe Book.* London: Dean & Munday, 1819.

Heaphy, Leslie A., and Mel Anthony May. *Encyclopedia of Women and Baseball.* Jefferson, NC: McFarland, 2006.

Higginbotham, Jay. *Mobile: City by the Bay.* Mobile, AL: Mobile Junior Chamber of Commerce, 1968.

———. *Old Mobile Fort Louis de la Louisiane 1702–1711.* Mobile, AL: Museum of the City of Mobile, 1977.

Hinson, Billy. *Mobile: A New History of Alabama's First City.* Tuscaloosa: University of Alabama Press, 2001.

Hubbs, G. Ward. *Searching for Freedom After the Civil War: Klansman, Carpetbagger, Scalawag.* Tuscaloosa: University of Alabama Press, 2015.

Inge, George B. *Our Book of State-Facts, Customs, Traditions, Biographies, Events and Anecdotes Pertaining to the Order of Myths.* Mobile, AL: Southern Lithographing Company, 1968.

Jones, John B. *Civil War 150 * Reader # 6: The War at Home.* New York: Library of America, 1962.

Kiple, Kenneth F., and Kriemhild Conee Ornelas. *The Cambridge World History of Food.* Cambridge, UK: Cambridge University Press, 2000.

Kloeppel, James E. *Danger Beneath the Waves: A History of the Confederate Submarine* H.L. Hunley. College Park, FL: Adele Enterprises, 1987.

Marx, Harpo. *Harpo Speaks!* Lanham, MD: Limelight Editions, 1961.

McWilliams, Richebourg Gaillard. *Fleur de Lys and Calumet: Being the Penicaut Narrative of French Adventure in Louisiana.* Tuscaloosa: University of Alabama Press, 1953.

Nemec, David. *Major League Baseball Profiles, 1871–1900: The Ballplayers Who Built the Game.* Lincoln, NE: Bison Books, 2011.

Pillens, Palmer. *Mobile in Two Centuries as Remembered by Palmer Pillans.* Tuscaloosa: University of Alabama Press, 1970.

Pond, Ann J. *Cowbellion: The Origins of America's Mystic Mardi Gras.* Seattle, WA: Amazon Digital Services, 2015.

———. *Masons & Mardi Gras.* N.p., Lulu.com, 2015.

Ragan, Mark K. *Confederate Saboteurs: Building the* Hunley *and Other Secret Weapons of the Civil War*. College Station: Texas A&M University Press, 2015.

Ravesies, Paul. *Scenes and Settlers of Alabama*. Lebanon, TN: Franklin Classics, 2018.

Roberts, L. Craig. *Mardi Gras in Mobile*. Charleston, SC: The History Press, 2015.

Government Publications

Baker, Benjamin D. *Mobile Park's Iron Deer Is Survivor of the War Between the States*, Washington, D.C.: Federal Writers Program Miscellaneous Essays Concerning the History and Legends of Mobile and Mobile County, November 7, 1939.

———. *Mobile's Fire Lads of 1819*. Washington, D.C.: Federal Writers Program Miscellaneous Essays Concerning the History and Legends of Mobile and Mobile County, December 6, 1939.

———. *Phantom Ship of Belle Fountaine Fortells Coming Storm, Says Legend*. Washington, D.C.: Federal Writers Program Miscellaneous Essays Concerning the History and Legends of Mobile and Mobile County, December 15, 1939.

———. *Recalls Days When Ice Came Down from Maine by Ships*. Washington, D.C.: Federal Writer's Program Miscellaneous Essays Concerning the History and Legends of Mobile and Mobile County, November 6, 1939.

———. *Russian Czar's Wife Was Alleged to Have Found Peace and Happiness Here*. Washington, D.C.: Federal Writer's Program Miscellaneous Essays Concerning the History and Legends of Mobile and Mobile County, December 6, 1939.

General Assembly of Alabama Passed at the Session of 1888–1889. Montgomery, AL: Barrett & Company, 1819–1897.

Library of Congress. *New FCC Commissioner Takes Oath* by Harris and Ewing, Photographer, Washington, D.C., 1939. http://www.loc.gov/item/2016875437.

Rees, Susan Ivester. *Final Environmental Impact Statement for Choctaw Point Terminal Project*. Mobile, AL: U.S. Army Corps of Engineers, 2004.

U.S. Census Bureau. *Population of the 100 Largest Cities and Other Urban Places in the United States: 1790 to 1990*. Washington, D.C., 1998. www.census.gov/population/www/documentation/twps0027/twps0027.html.

Journal and Presentation References

Johnson, Mrs. "Augusta Evans Wilson: A Paper Given by Mrs. Johnson at the October 1956 Meeting of the New Idea Study Club." Paper presented at the October 1956 meeting of the New Idea Study Club, Mobile, AL, 1956. Mobile Public Library Local History and Genealogy.

Knight, Vernon J., and Sheree L. Adams, "A Voyage to the Mobile and Tomeh in 1700, with Notes on the Interior of Alabama." *American Society for Ethnohistory* 28, no. 2 (Spring 1981): 179–82.

Magazine and Newspaper References

AL.com and Register Staff. "Mobile Press-Register 200th Anniversary: A Timeline of Mobile's Newspaper."

Bank advertisement. "Frascatti, Where Time Bears Witness to Sound Building." Mobile Public Library Local History and Genealogy, date unknown.

Biloxi Daily Herald. "Deputy Easterling Is Shot Dead in Mobile." March 1, 1921.

Book Mart. "Augusta Evans Wilson." March 1918, page 259.

Brackner, Joey. "The Excelsior Band Leading the Parade for 125 Years." *Alabama Arts* 25, no. 1 (2013): 44–47.

Bryars, Dianne. "A Rebel's Legacy." *Azalea City News and Review*, March 2, 1988.

Davis, Linda A.B. "Southern Perspective: French Casket Girls Helped Shape the South." *Pensacola News Journal*, January 12, 2018.

East, Cammie. "'Notorious' Depicts This Pirate of 1800s." *Mobile Press Register*, May 14, 1984.

————. "Ship Ahoy, Lads! Up wi' Jolly Roger!" *Mobile Press Register*, May 14, 1984.

Erskine, James A. "Frascati Information: Historic Building Renovated by Illinois Central Gulf Railroad." *Mobile Public Library Local History and Genealogy* (January 1975).

Fidler, William Perry. "Augusta Evans Wilson as Confederate Propagandist." *Alabama Review* (January 1949): 32.

Fulton, Imogen Inge. "Frascati: A Vignette of History." *Mobile Register*, October 17, 1993.

Hickerson, Patrick. "Experts Closing in on Site of Bloody Battle of Mabila." AL.com, September 13, 2009.

Hicks, Tommy. "Dolly White, Former Player in Women's League, in a League of Her Own." AL.com, January 14, 2011.

Hotel and Restaurant Employees International Alliance. "Car Load of Intoxicants Seized in the Principal Hotels of Mobile." *Mixer & Server* 18, no. 5 (May 1909): 43.

Jansen, Holly. "Line Drives and Lipstick." *Mobile Bay Monthly* (April 2013).

Jones, Pam. "Alabama Mysteries." *Alabama Heritage*, no. 78 (Fall 2005). https://www.alabamaheritage.com.

Kazek, Kelly. "'Arrrr' There Pirate Tales from Alabama?" *Mobile Press Register*, September 22, 2013.

————. "Louisiana Again Claiming 1st Mardi Gras; Here's the Case for Mobile." AL.com, February 1, 2018.

————. "On Repeal Day 7 Places Alabamians Bought Illicit Liquor During Prohibition." AL.com, December 5, 2014.

————. "On This Day in 1807, Aaron Burr Was Arrested in Alabama." AL.com, February 19, 2015.

————. "When French Orphans Called Casket Girls Came to Alabama as Wives for Colonists." AL.com, September, 14, 2015.

Kirby, Brenden. "Boardwalk Empire of the South: Prohibition Brought Violence, Corruption to Mobile." AL.com, June 23, 2013.

————. "Depression Crushes Mobile, but It Could Have Been Worse." AL.com, June 24, 2013.

Largue, Laren. "ELVIS! The Early Years." *Mobile Bay Monthly* (July 2011).

Laurence, Jacob. "The Swashbucklers." *Mobile Bay Monthly* (January 2009): 80–83.

Lineback, Neal, and Mandy Lineback Gritzner. "Geography in the News: Hernando De Soto's Famous Battle." *National Geographic*, June 14, 2014. https://blog.nationalgeographic.org.

McFadyen, Chris. "The Great Bootleg Conspiracy of 1924." *Mobile Bay Monthly* 8, no. 2 (March 1993): 21.

Milwaukee Sentinel. "Dry Alabama Moonshine Leader." January 18, 1937.

Mobile Daily Register. "An Opportunity for a Public Park." Mobile Public Library Local History and Genealogy, no date or page.

————. "Frascati Sold." Sunday, May 24, 1891.

————. "Western Shore. A Sunday Tour to South End." July 1, 1885.

Mobile Register. "Augusta Evans Wilson Buried in Magnolia." May 11, 1909.

————. "Augusta Evans Wilson in Time of War." May 10, 1909.

————. "Augusta Evans Wilson, Noted Novelist, Is Dead." May 10, 1909.

————. "Deputy Tells of Raids on Shinny Makers by Force." December 5, 1920.

————. "Dry Law Aid Held Needed by Sargent." January 28, 1916.

————. "Liquor Is Doomed in Alabama." January 13, 1915.

————. "Mobilian Smashed $100,000 Barrier of Women Writers; Books Still Sell." July 29, 1962.

————. "Mobilians Taken in Raid of U.S. Agents." November 14, 1923.

————. "Oscar Wilde." June 28, 1882.

————. "Prohibition Law Pushed Through House and Senate." January 15, 1915.

————. "Prohibitionists Are in Control of Both Houses." January 12, 1915.

————. "Prohibitionists in Control of Both Houses." January 28, 1926.

————. "U.S. Men Swoop Down on Liquor Traffic Here." November 14, 1923.

Mobile Register and Advertiser. "Arrest of Ellen Bosquis." September 12, 1861.

————. "An Excellent Substitute for Coffee." October 9, 1861.

————. "Mobile Bread Riot." September 5, 1863.

Mobile Weekly Tribune. "Water for Firemen." March 19, 1870.

National Association Practical Refrigerating Engineers. "Owing to the Enforcement of Prohibition at Mobile, Ala." *Ice and Refrigeration Illustrated* 38, no. 1 (January 1910): 121.

New Orleans Era. "Two Outbreaks in One Day. Arrivals in the City." October 1, 1863.

New York Times. "Alabama and Prohibition." December 4, 1909.

Rogers, William Warren, Dorothy McLeod MacInerney and Robert David Ward. "The Wilde Alabama Lecture Circuit." *Alabama Heritage* no. 78 (Fall 2005): 6–13.

Rogers, William Warren, and Rober Davis Ward. "An Aesthete at Large: Oscar Wilde in Mobile." *Gulf Coast Historical Review* (Spring 1991): 49.

Sledge, John. "Encounter Mobile Bay's Notorious Piratical Scoundrel." *Mobile Bay Monthly* (December 2018).

Snelson, Floyd G. "Four Pretty Girls Female Edition of Mills Brothers?" *Pittsburgh Courier*, January 28, 1933.

Stevenson, Tommy. "At Large: The Holy Grail of Southern Archaeology." *Tuscaloosa News*, October 17, 2014.

Times-Picayune. "John Scott, Alias John Carney." June 28, 1840.

Trenier, Mark. "Creole Fire Company No. 1." *Mumbo Gumbo* (Spring 2019): 5.

Webb, Samuel L. "Whiskey War." *Alabama Heritage* (Spring 2005): 30.

Williams, Benjamin B. "Augusta Evans Wilson (1835–1909)." *Landmark Letter* 23, no. 2 (Fall 1990).

Video References

Kern, Jackson. "The Pope Sisters Interview Clip." National African American Archives & Museum, Museum of Mobile, Mobile Public Library, Local History & Genealogy. Video File. 2000. http://digital.mobilepubliclibrary.org/items/show/2190.

Website References

AAGPBL editors. "Margaret Silvestri." All American Girls Professional Baseball League, www.aagpbl.org.

Alicia T. "Pope Sisters." Internet Movie Database. www.imdb.com.

Baseball Almanac. "Charlie Duffee Stats." www.baseball-almanac.com.

Baseball Farming editors. "Alabama-Players-MLB: Major League Baseball Welcomed the Native Sons of Alabama." baseballfarming.com.

Baseball Reference. "Charlie Duffee." baseballreference.com.

Biography editors. "Alexander Hamilton." biography.com.

Brackner, Joey. "The Excelsior Marching Band (2013)." Alabama State Council of the Arts, arts.alabama.gov.

Branley, Edward. "History of the Casket Girls of New Orleans." Go Nola, October 16, 2018, gonola.com.

Causey, Donna R. "The French Sent Young Girls to Marry in Alabama in 1719." Alabama Pioneers, www.alabamapioneers.com.

CBS News Staff Writers. "Deadliest Storms in U.S. History." CBS News, www.cbsnews.com.

Cook, David A., and Robert Sklar. "History of the Motion Picture." Encyclopædia Brittanica, www.britannica.com.

Davis, Angela D. "Excelsior Band." *New Times Weekly*, February 11, 1988. www.alabamamusicoffice.com

Downs, Matthew L. "Great Depression in Alabama," Encyclopedia of Alabama, July 10, 2014. www.encyclopediaofalabama.org.

Duncan, Matthew. "Curtis Gordon." Alabama Music Office, May 2004. www.alabamamusicoffice.com.

Find a Grave editors. "Odile Pope Owen." Find a Grave, www.findagrave.com.

Fleming, Frank. "Columbus Solons." Sports Encyclopedia, July 4, 2017. sportsecyclopedia.com.

Genealogy Bank editors. "Mobile Register (Mobile, Alabama) Newspaper Archives (1833–2003)." www.genealogybank.com.

Geni editors. "Casket Girls." www.geni.com.

Ghost City Tours editors. "The Truth about the Ursuline Casket Girls of New Orleans." ghostcitytours.com.

Gracyk, Tim. "Songs Brought Back from the Battlefield." www.redhotjazz.com.

Gu, Mike. "Mobile, Alabama, 1930s–1940s," Prezi, https://prezi.com.

Hall, Christie Matherne. "Cheniere Caminada's 'Great October Storm.'" *Country Roads Magazine*, September 27, 2016. https://countryroadsmagazine.com.

History editors. "Aaron Burr Arrested for Treason." www.history.com.

History Central editors. "Clothing in Antebellum America." www.historycentral.com.

Hurricane Research Division Historians. "The 125th Anniversary of the Cheniere Caminada Hurricane." NOAA, October 2, 2018. https://noaahrd.wordpress.com.

Inabinett, Mark. "Charlie Duffee Got Something Started for Alabama 125 Years Ago Today." AL.com, April 17, 2014. www.al.com.

Keyes, Pam. "Paddy Scott: The Irish Pirate who Plagued Mobile." Historia Obscura, January 30, 2016. www.historiaobscura.com.

Kirkland, Scotty E. "Mobile." Encyclopedia of Alabama, September 25, 2008. www.encyclopediaofalabama.org.

———. "Mobile Bread Riot." Encyclopedia of Alabama, November 13, 2013. www.encyclopediaofalabama.org.

Kittel, Jeffrey. "This Game of Games: Exploring the History of 19th Century St. Louis Baseball." This Game of Games, December 1, 2007. http://thisgameofgames.blogspot.com.

Lanham, Jenni. "Mobile, AL Hurricane, Oct 1893—Damage." GenDisasters, www.gendisasters.com.

Library of Congress. "African American Performers on Early Sound Recordings, 1892–1916." www.loc.gov.

———. "James Reese Europe." www.loc.gov.

McGehee, Tom. "A Hurricane to Remember: The Tragic 1906 Storm That Struck Mobile." Bellingrath Gardens, https://bellingrath.org.

Monet, Delores. "Women's Clothing of the South in the Civil War." Bellatory, July 30, 2017. https://bellatory.com.

Moore, Scotty. "Til I Found Myself in Mobile, Alabama at Ladd Stadium." Scotty More, the Official Website, December 5, 2008. www.scottymoore.net.

Morris, Melinda. "The No-Name Hurricane of 1893." Nola.com, October 1, 2018. https://expo.nola.com.

National Hurricane Center and Pacific Hurricane Center. "Tropical Cyclone Naming History and Retired Names." NOAA, www.nhc.noaa.gov.

National Weather Service. "History of NWS Mobile / Pensacola." NOAA, www.weather.gov.

Obituary Staff Writers. "Una Tuttle." AL.Com, https://obits.al.com.

Otte, Katherine. "The Seven Most Infamous Pirate Queens." The Odd Historian, August 8, 2017. www.oddhistorian.com.

Paul, Kris. "The History of St. Louis Baseball-Part 6: The Player's Revolt (1890)." www.krispaulw.com/baseball/history/part06.html.

Poore, Ralph. "The Mobile Press-Register." Encyclopedia of Alabama, January 8, 2008. http://encyclopediaofalabama.org.

Price, Gary. "Charles Melvin 'Cootie' Williams." *Syncopated Times*, July 1, 2017. https://syncopatedtimes.com.

Ray, Micheal. "James Reese Europe." Encyclopædia Brittanica, www.britannica.com.

Sealls, Alan. "Mobile's Hurricane History;" WKRG-TV, January 12, 2018, www.wkrg.com.

Serpents of Bienville. "Your Invitation, Ma'am;" www.serpentsofbienville.com;

Soul Walking Editors. "The Treniers," Soulwalking, www.soulwalking.co.uk.

Tabler, Dave. "Prohibition Comes to Alabama. Again." Appalachian History, June 12, 2019. www.appalachianhistory.net.

Thornley, Stew. "Minnesota's First Major League Baseball Game." Stew Thornley, http://stewthornley.net.

Travis, Dave. "Curtis Gordon." Rockabilly Hall of Fame, www.rockabillyhall.com.

Uhlin, Mikael. "Fun in Hi Skule." The Marx Brothers, www.marx-brothers.org.

———. "Nightingales and Mascots." The Marx Brothers, www.marx-brothers.org.

"Vaudeville." Encyclopædia Brittanica, www.britannica.com.

Wilkinson, Tony, and Dave Travis. "Gordon, Curtis." Rockabilly Hall of Fame, www.rockabillyhall.com.

About the Author

J oe Cuhaj is a former radio broadcaster turned author and freelance writer. He began his radio career just outside of New York City but moved to Mobile in 1981 with his wife, who is from the Port City. His radio career flourished as he picked up a job at WUNI, which was originally the first radio station in Mobile, WODX.

Joe fell in love with Alabama's biodiversity and continued his favorite pastimes, hiking and backpacking. In 2000, he combined his love of hiking and writing and penned his first book, *Hiking Alabama*. Since then, Joe has written seven outdoor recreation books for Falcon Guides.

Joe left radio and became a software programmer but continued his passion for writing. In addition to outdoor recreation, Joe has a love and passion for history, which he had a chance to delve into when he coauthored *Baseball in Mobile* for Arcadia Publishing. He has also written historical articles and web content for several sites and publications on a wide variety of subjects, and falling back on his radio career, he has produced a number of humorous short story podcasts that can be heard on his website, www.joecuhaj.com.

Visit us at
www.historypress.com